Illustrated

Bicycle Trails
of
Illinois

An American Bike Trails Publication

Bicycle Trails
of Illinois

Published by   American Bike Trails
1157 S. Milwaukee Avenue
Libertyville, IL 60048

Created by   Ray Hoven
Design by   Mary C. Rumpsa

Table of Contents

Table of Contents

Selected Illinois State Parks

Indexes

How To Use This Book

T his book provides a comprehensive, easy-to-use quick reference to the many off-road trails throughout Illinois. It contains over 80 detailed trail maps, plus overviews covering the state sectionally, selective counties and city areas. Detail trail maps are listed alphabetically. The sectional overviews are grouped near the front, with a section cross-referencing counties and towns to trails, and a section listing many of the parks in Illinois with their pertinent information. Each trail map includes such helpful features as location and access, trail facilities, nearby communities and their populations.

Terms Used

Length Expressed in miles. Round trip mileage is normally indicated for loops.

Effort Levels *Easy* Physical exertion is not strenuous. Climbs and descents as well as technical obstacles are more minimal. Recommended for beginners.

Moderate Physical exertion is not excessive. Climbs and descents can be challenging. Expect some technical obstacles.

Difficult Physical exertion is demanding. Climbs and descents require good riding skills. Trail surface may be sandy, loose rock, soft or wet.

Directions Describes by way of directions and distances, how to get to the trail areas from roads and nearby communities.

Map Illustrative representation of a geographic area, such as a state, section, forest, park or trail complex.

Forest Typically encompasses a dense growth of trees and underbrush covering a large tract.

Park A tract of land generally including woodlands and open areas.

DNR Department of Natural Resources

Types of Biking

Mountain Fat-tired bikes are recommended. Ride may be generally flat but then with a soft, rocky or wet surface.

Leisure Off-road gentle ride. Surface is generally paved or screened.

Tour Riding on roads with motorized traffic or on road shoulders.

Riding Tips

☐ Pushing in gears that are too high can push knees beyond their limits. Avoid extremes by pedaling faster rather than shifting into a higher gear.

☐ Keeping your elbows bent, changing your hand position frequently and wearing bicycle gloves all help to reduce the numbness or pain in the palm of the hand from long-distance riding.

☐ Keep you pedal rpms up on an uphill so you have reserve power if you lose speed.

☐ Stay in a high-gear on a level surface, placing pressure on the pedals and resting on the handle bars and saddle.

☐ Lower your center of gravity on a long or steep downhill run by using the quick release seat post binder and dropping the saddle height down.

☐ Brake intermittently on a rough surface.

☐ Wear proper equipment. Wear a helmet that is approved by the Snell Memorial Foundation or the American National Standards Institute. Look for one of their stickers inside the helmet.

☐ Use a lower tire inflation pressure for riding on unpaved surfaces. The lower pressure will provide better tire traction and a more comfortable ride.

☐ Apply your brakes gradually to maintain control on loose gravel or soil.

☐ Ride only on trails designated for bicycles or in areas where you have the permission of the landowner.

☐ Be courteous to hikers or horseback riders on the trail, they have the right of way.

☐ Leave riding trails in the condition you found them. Be sensitive to the environment. Properly dispose of your trash. If you open a gate, close it behind you.

☐ Don't carry items or attach anything to your bicycle that might hinder your vision or control.

☐ Don't wear anything that restricts your hearing.

☐ Don't carry extra clothing where it can hang down and jam in a wheel.

Explanation of Symbols

ROUTES

▬▬▬▬	Biking Trail
▬ ▬ ▬	Bikeway
─ ─ ─	Alternate Bike Trail
▬ ▬ ▬	Alternate Use Trail
= = =	Planned Trail
▬▬▬▬	Roadway

TRAIL USES

🚵	Mountain Biking
🚲	Leisure Biking
⛸	In Line Skating
⛷	(X-C) Cross-Country Skiing
🚶	Hiking
⋂	Horseback Riding
🛷	Snowmobiling

FACILITIES

🔧	Bike Repair
⛺	Camping
➕	First Aid
❓	Info
🛏	Lodging
🅿	Parking
🎪	Picnic
🍽	Refreshments
🚻	Restrooms
🏠	Shelter
🚰	Water
MF	Multi Facilities Available

Refreshments	First Aid
Telephone	Picnic
Restrooms	Lodging

ROAD RELATED SYMBOLS

(45)	Interstate Highway
(45)	U.S. Highway
(45)	State Highway
45	County Highway

AREA DESCRIPTIONS

▢	Parks, Schools, Preserves, etc.
▢	Waterway
▭	Mileage Scale
W-⊕-E	Directional

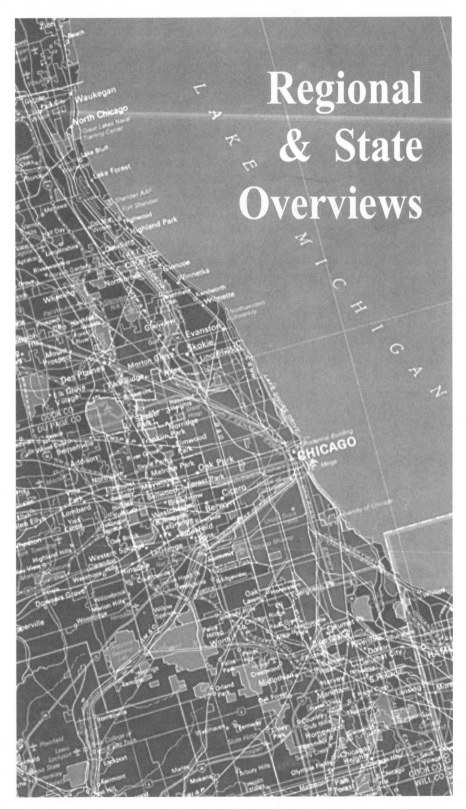

Regional
& State
Overviews

State of Illinois

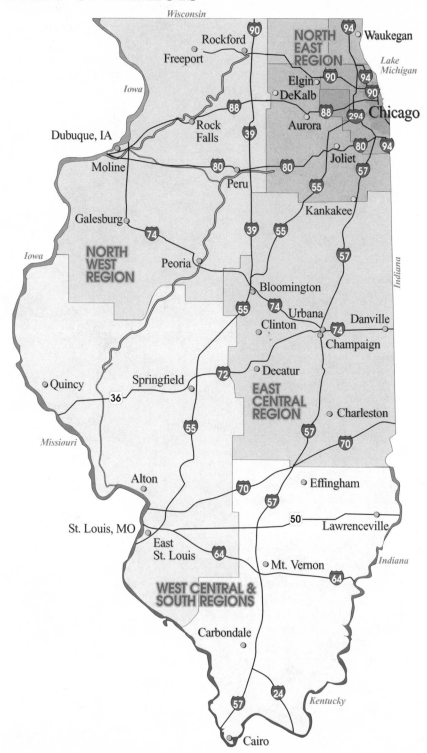

Wisconsin

Rockford
Freeport

NORTH
EAST
REGION

Waukegan

Lake
Michigan

Iowa

Elgin
DeKalb

Rock
Falls

Aurora

Chicago

Dubuque, IA

Moline

Peru

Joliet

Galesburg

NORTH
WEST
REGION

Peoria

Kankakee

Iowa

Bloomington

Indiana

Clinton

Urbana

Danville

Quincy

Springfield

Decatur

Champaign

EAST
CENTRAL
REGION

Charleston

Missouri

Alton

Effingham

St. Louis, MO

East
St. Louis

Lawrenceville

Mt. Vernon

Indiana

WEST CENTRAL &
SOUTH REGIONS

Carbondale

Kentucky

Cairo

MILEAGE BETWEEN PRINCIPAL CITIES

CITY	SPRINGFIELD	ST. LOUIS, MO	ROCKFORD	PEORIA	CHICAGO	CHAMPAIGN
BLOOMINGTON	64	163	136	40	136	53
CAIRO	242	148	426	312	375	244
CARBONDALE	172	108	384	242	333	202
CHAMPAIGN	86	182	188	92	137	
CHICAGO	201	300	83	170		137
DECATUR	39	118	179	83	178	47
DE KALB	183	282	44	124	66	174
DUBUQUE, IA	238	337	91	167	176	259
EFFINGHAM	89	104	260	164	209	78
ELGIN	208	307	48	148	37	169
GALESBURG	120	219	150	49	198	141
KANKAKEE	158	254	138	121	56	78
LAWRENCEVILLE	154	147	309	213	250	127
MOLINE	163	262	117	92	165	184
MT. VERNON	146	82	330	216	279	148
PEORIA	71	170	138		170	92
QUINCY	110	133	269	131	310	195
ROCKFORD	197	296		138	83	188
ST. LOUIS, MO	100		296	170	300	182
SPRINGFIELD		100	197	71	201	86
WAUKEGAN	229	328	71	198	40	181

State of Illinois

North West Region

Bicycle Resources

ACCESS ILLINOIS (COMPUTER SOFTWARE)
Free

Modem access number
(217) 787-6255
Technical assistance
(217) 698-9003

Set communications software to 8 (Data Bits), N (Parity), 1 (Stop Bits) and ANSI text. This on-line service allows users to access information about Illinois tourism, government, and special events, including bicycling events.

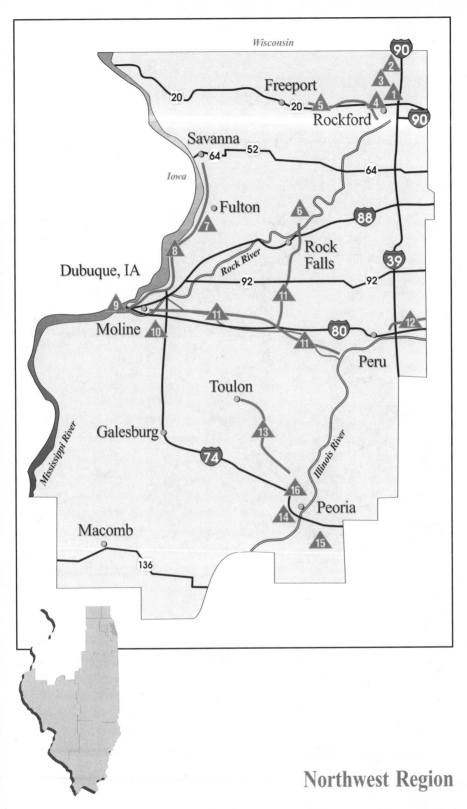

Northwest Region

North East Region

Riding the Cook County Trails

Planning for that Trail Visit

Checkoff List

Information you may want to have at hand

- ☐ Trail location
- ☐ Trail accesses
- ☐ Parking
- ☐ Restrooms
- ☐ Drinking water
- ☐ Refreshments
- ☐ Lodging
- ☐ Conditions
- ☐ Local area events
- ☐ Telephone access
- ☐ Bicycle service
- ☐ Picnic facilities
- ☐ Shelters
- ☐ Camping facilities
- ☐ Emergency assistance phone number

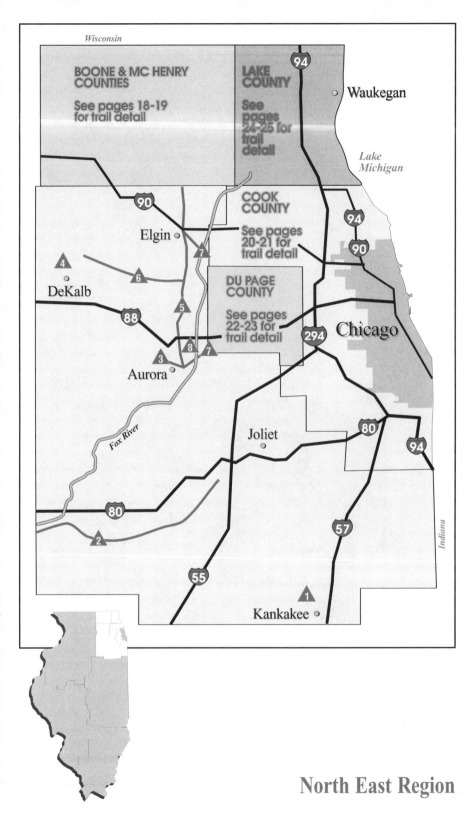

North East Region

East Central Region

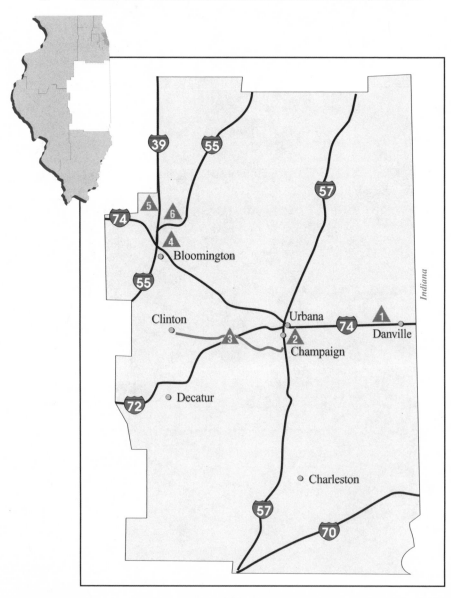

West Central and South Regions

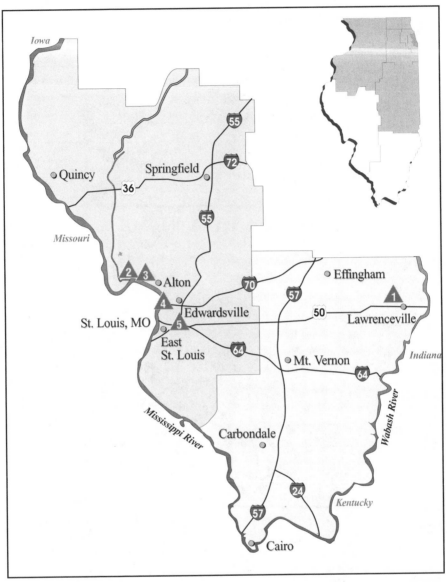

Boone and McHenry Counties

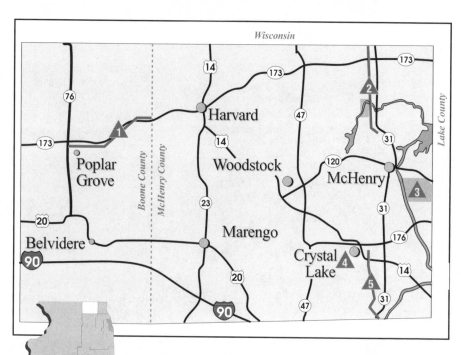

American Bike Trails publishes bicycle trail maps and books covering Illinois and surrounding states. For more information or a free catalog write to:

American Bike Trails
1157 South Milwaukee Avenue
Libertyville, IL 60048

Disappearing Ducks

Historically the Illinois River's backwater lakes have been among the most important migration areas for several species of ducks, including mallards. Since 1948, however, significantly fewer migrating mallards have alighted in the Illinois valley each fall. The trend is thought to reflect the general decline in mallard numbers across North America, but there is evidence that local conditions also have deteriorated.

The Illinois River's complex system of wetlands has long attracted more mallards than that of the Mississippi River. (In the late 1940s, mallards along the Illinois outnumbered those sojourning on the larger river nine to one.) The post-1948 decline in mallard counts along the Illinois has been relatively steeper than that recorded on the Mississippi, where sedimentation has not caused such drastic reductions in the amount and variety of natural plant foods available to migrating flocks. In addition, tillage of increased acreage of harvested corn fields in central Illinois during fall sharply decreased the waste grain available to the field-feeding mallards.

Two other duck species—the lesser scaup and the canvasback—have suffered more drastic population crashes on the Illinois River. Lesser scaups were abundant in the Illinois valley before the 1950s, especially on Upper Peoria Lake. More than 585,000 ducks were counted on one stretch of the river in 1954; three years later the number was around 10,000. Similar trends were recorded in populations of canvasbacks. During the 1952 migration more than 105,000 birds were counted along the Illinois River north of Peoria; in 1971, only 120 were seen.

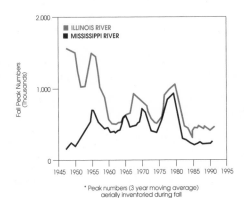

* Peak numbers (3 year moving average)
aerially inventoried during fall

The cause of the decline in numbers of lesser scaup and canvasback ducks in the Illinois River valley is a scarcity of food. The rafts of aquatic vegetation that used to sustain the canvasback flocks on the Upper Peoria Lake have disappeared as a result of sedimentation (which causes turbid water and flocculent lakebeds) and changes in seasonal water level cycles. Also the benthic macroinvertebrate community—the small clams and other bottom dwelling creatures especially crucial to diving ducks like the lesser scaup—was likely affected by sedimentation and pollution from various domestic, industrial, and agricultural sources.

Cook County

The Natural Landscape of Illinois

The natural landscape can be divided into 14 divisions, based on topography, glacial history, bedrock, soils, and distribution of plants and animals. Various kinds of prairies occurred in each of these natural divisions. The 1978 Natural Areas Inventory recognizes six main subclasses of prairie including:

black soil prairie   **sand prairie**   **gravel prairie**

dolomite prairie   **hill prairie**   **shrub prairie**

Along the shores of Lake Michigan and the Illinois, Kankakee, and Mississippi rivers, are extensive sand deposits, often forming dunes or ridges and swales, and several kinds of sand prairies can be found in such areas. Hill prairies are found on dry, southwest-facing, loess-covered hill tops above bluffs overlooking floodplains of rivers, especially the Illinois and Mississippi Rivers. In northeastern Illinois some distinctive prairie vegetation can be found in very wet alkaline fens and marl flats.

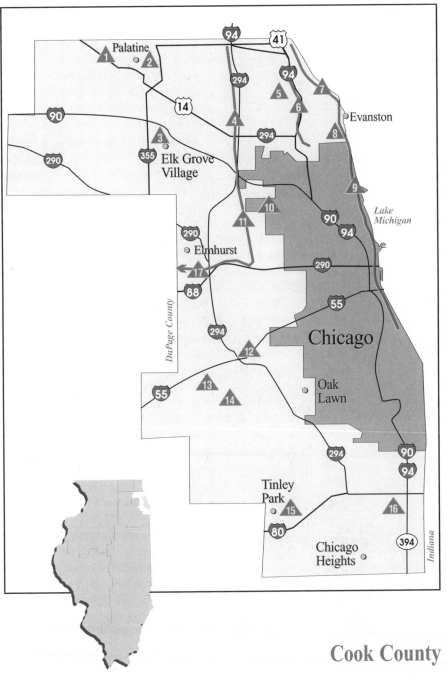

Cook County

DuPage County

Bicycle Resources

BICYCLING *(BROCHURE)*
Free
Illinois Department of Conservation
Office of Resource Marketing and Education
524 South Second Street
Springfield, IL 62701-1787

(217)782-7454

Information brochure listing off-road bicycle trails statewide. The Department of Conservation also distributes an attractive Illinois State Parks magazine as well as brochures on hiking, camping, and other outdoor activities.

ILLINOIS VISITOR'S GUIDE
Illinois Dept. of Commerce and Community Affairs
Bureau of Tourism
620 East Adams Street
Springfield, IL 62701

(800)223-0121

Lists campgrounds, hotels and motels, and recreational and cultural attractions throughout the state.

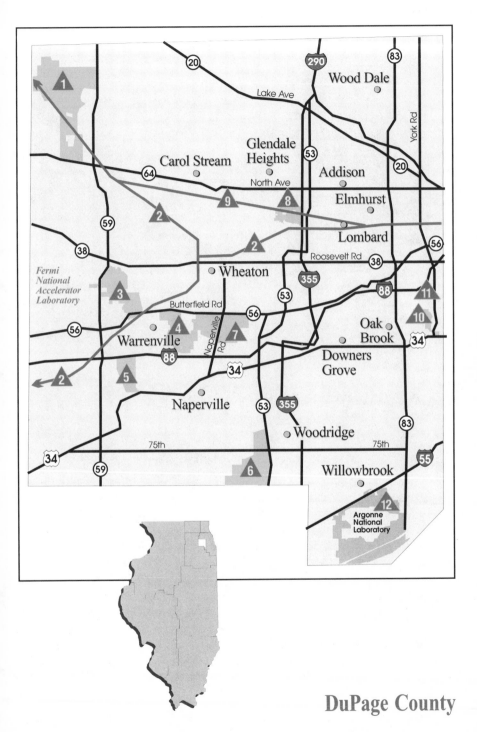

Fermi National Accelerator Laboratory

Carol Stream

Glendale Heights

Wood Dale

Addison

Elmhurst

Lombard

Wheaton

Warrenville

Oak Brook

Downers Grove

Naperville

Woodridge

Willowbrook

Argonne National Laboratory

Lake Ave

North Ave

Roosevelt Rd

Butterfield Rd

Naperville Rd

75th

75th

York Rd

DuPage County

Lake County

Bicycle Resources

BIKE TOURING INFORMATION

The State of Illinois recommends that when planning a bike tour the Department of Transportation be contacted for county maps showing low-volume local roads along your selected route. A map catalog can be obtained from:

Map Sales
Illinois Dept. of Transportation
2300 South Dirksen Parkway
Springfield, IL 62764

For more information concerning other trail activities, please contact:

Illinois Department of Conservation
Office of Public Information
524 South 2nd Street
Springfield, IL 62701-1787

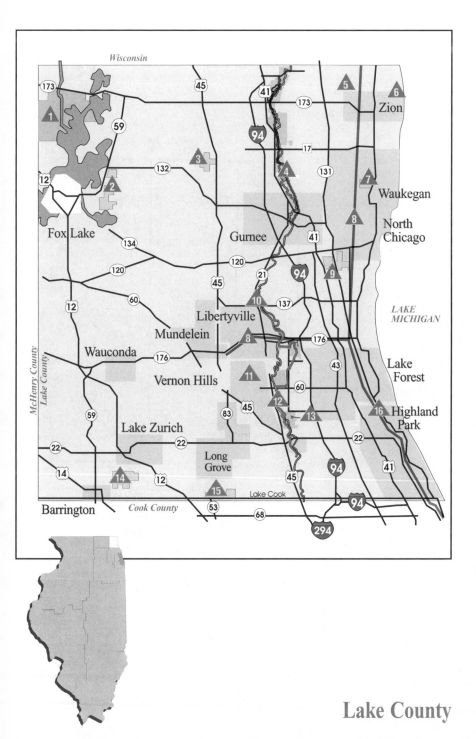

Wisconsin

173

45

41

5

6

173

Zion

1

59

94

17

132

3

4

131

7

12

2

Waukegan

134

Gurnee

8

North
Chicago

Fox Lake

120

41

120

45

21

94

9

LAKE
MICHIGAN

60

10

137

12

Libertyville

Mundelein

8

176

Lake
Forest

Wauconda

176

43

Vernon Hills

11

60

59

83

45

12

Lake Zurich

22

13

16

Highland
Park

22

22

94

41

14

Long
Grove

14

12

15

Lake Cook

45

94

Barrington

Cook County

53

68

94

294

McHenry County

Lake County

Lake County

Rockford Area

Information   Rockford Park District
(815) 987-8865
1401 N. Second Street
Rockford, IL 61107-3086

County   Winnebago

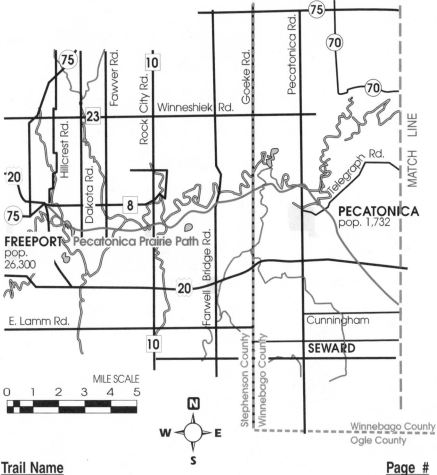

MILE SCALE

0 1 2 3 4 5

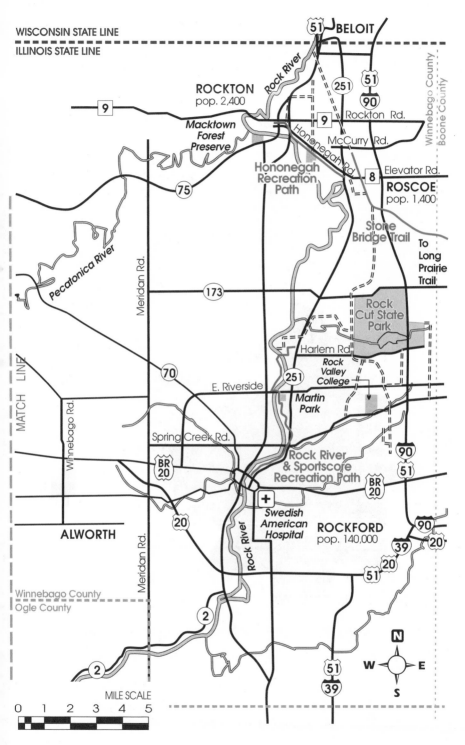

Rockford Area

To order additional copies of this book:

Pay by Check or Credit Card

Mail Check to:

American Bike Trails
1157 South Milwaukee Avenue
Libertyville, IL 60048

Book *(per copy)* $14.95
Handling *(per order)* $2.00
Sales Tax—IL residents *(per copy)* $1.00

To order by Credit Card call (800) 246-4627

American Bike Trails
publishes and distributes maps, books and guides
for the recreational bicyclist. Our trail maps
cover over 250 trails throughout the states of
Illinois, Iowa, Michigan, Minnesota and Wisconsin.

For a free copy of our catalog write to the above address

Trails

Arie Crown Bicycle Trail

Trail Length	3.2 miles
Surface	Paved
Uses	Leisure bicycling, in-line skating, cross country skiing, jogging
Location & Setting	Located in south Cook County near Countryside and north of the Palos Forest Preserve. Access at Brainard and Joliet Roads or LaGrange Road, north of 67th Street. Woods, open areas.
Information	Forest Preserve District of Cook County (708) 366-8420 536 N. Harlem Avenue River Forest, IL 60305
County	Cook

EMERGENCY ASSISTANCE
Forest Preserve Police   (708) 366-8210
                       or   (708) 366-8211

ROUTES

— Bicycling Trail
--- Alternate Bike Trail
— Roadway

COUNTRYSIDE
pop. 6,500

Mannheim Rd

Joliet Rd

Entrance

N
W   E
S

Brainard Rd

12
20

Lake Ida

HODGKINS
pop. 2,000

Entrance

Entrance

P   67th St

INDIAN
HEAD
PARK
pop.
2,900

Willow Springs Rd

Entrance

P   MF

3.2 mi
total

Entrance

P

La Grange Rd

55   Stevenson Expy

MILE SCALE

0   ¼   ½   1

Blackwell Forest Preserve

Trail Length	3.3 miles leisure, 8.3 miles total
Surface	Limestone screenings, natural groomed
Uses	Leisure and fat tire bicycling.cross country skiing, hiking/jogging (horseback riding is restricted)
Location & Setting	The Blackwell Preserve, located between Winfield and Warrenville in west central DuPage County, can be accessed from Butterfield Road, 1 mile west of Route 59 or from Mack Road, ¼ miles east of Route 59.
Information	Forest Preserve District of DuPage County (630) 790-4900 185 Spring Avenue Glen Ellyn, IL 60138
County	DuPage

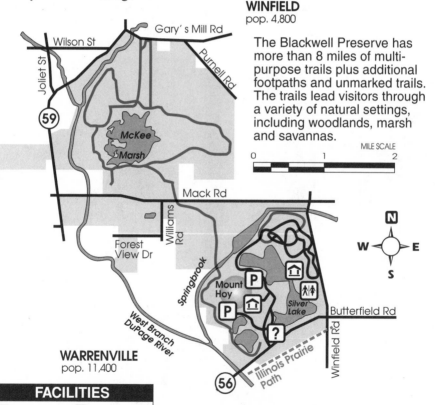

WINFIELD
pop. 4,800

The Blackwell Preserve has more than 8 miles of multi-purpose trails plus additional footpaths and unmarked trails. The trails lead visitors through a variety of natural settings, including woodlands, marsh and savannas.

MILE SCALE

WARRENVILLE
pop. 11,400

FACILITIES

? Info	🚻 Restrooms
P Parking	⌂ Shelter
MF Multi Facilities Available	

Refreshments First Aid Telephone
Picnic Restrooms Lodging

Bicyclists are encouraged to stay on the designated trails in the McKee Marsh area on the north end of the Preserve.

Busse Woods Bicycle Trail

Trail Length	11.2 miles
Surface	Paved
Uses	Leisure bicycling, in-line skating, cross country skiing, hiking/jogging
Location & Setting	Located in northwest Cook County in the Ned Brown Preserve, bordered on the north by Arlington Heights and to the east by Elk Grove Village. Wooded areas, open spaces and small lakes.
Information	Forest Preserve District of Cook County 536 N. Harlem Avenue (708) 366-9420 River Forest, IL 60305
County	Cook

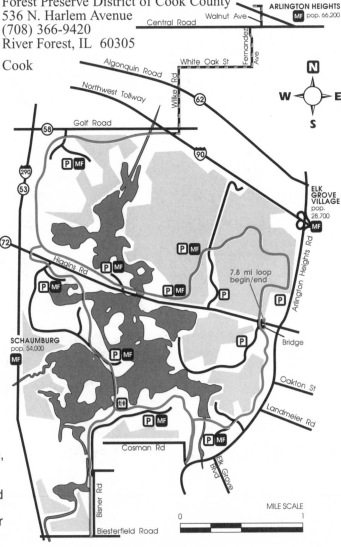

The Ned Brown Preserve is a 3,700 acre holding, and surrounds Busse Lake, a 590 acre lake that serves as the focal point of the area.

The bicycle trail winds through the forests and meadows around Busse Lake providing access to many of the preserves unique features.

Trail accesses include Golf Road at Hwy. 90, Arlington Heights Road and Higgins, and at Beisterfield Road and Bisner Road.

Chain O'Lakes State Park

Trail Length 5.0 miles

Surface Limestone screenings

Uses Leisure bicycling, cross country skiing, hiking, horseback riding

Location & Setting Chain O'Lakes State Park is a 2,793 acre park located at the northwest corner of Lake County. Woods, open park areas.

Information Chain O'Lakes State Park (847) 587-5512
39947 North State Park Road
Spring Grove, IL 60081

County Lake

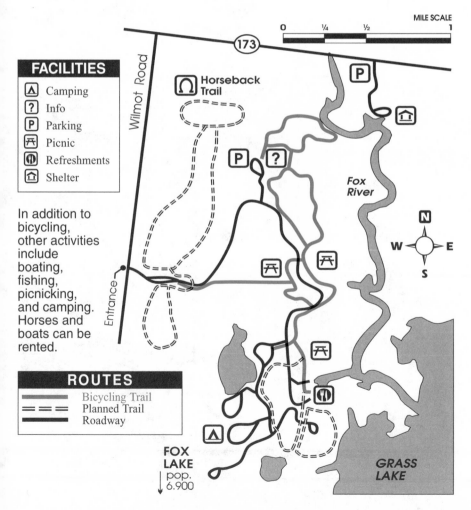

FACILITIES

- ⛺ Camping
- ？ Info
- Ｐ Parking
- 🛏 Picnic
- ◑ Refreshments
- 🏠 Shelter

In addition to bicycling, other activities include boating, fishing, picnicking, and camping. Horses and boats can be rented.

ROUTES

- ▬▬▬ Bicycling Trail
- ≡ ≡ ≡ Planned Trail
- ▬▬▬ Roadway

MILE SCALE

0   ¼   ½   1

Wilmot Road

🔸 Horseback Trail

Ｐ

🏠

Ｐ   ？

Fox River

N W E S

🛏   🛏

Entrance

🛏

◑

⛺

FOX LAKE
pop.
6,900

GRASS LAKE

Champaign County

Trail Length	Approximately 18 miles of bike path (plus over 30 miles of bike routes)
Surface	Paved
Uses	Leisure bicycling, in-line skating, hiking/jogging

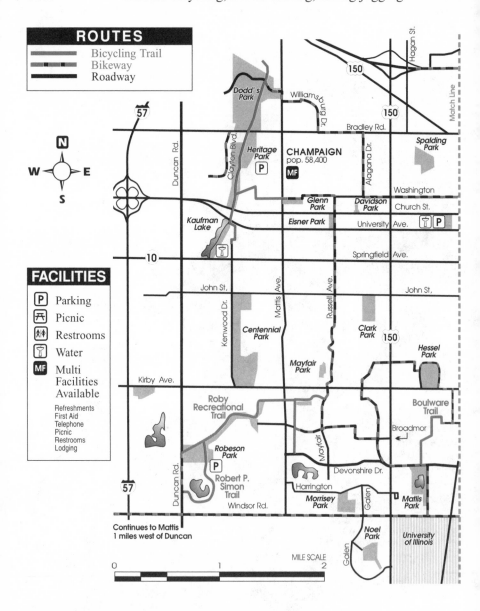

ROUTES
- Bicycling Trail
- Bikeway
- Roadway

FACILITIES
- P Parking
- Picnic
- Restrooms
- Water
- MF Multi Facilities Available

Refreshments
First Aid
Telephone
Picnic
Restrooms
Lodging

N
W E
S

150

Dodd's Park

Williamsburg Dr.

150

Bradley Rd.

Spalding Park

Duncan Rd.

Clayton Blvd.

Heritage Park
P

CHAMPAIGN
pop. 58,400
MF

Alagana Dr.

Washington

Glenn Park

Davidson Park

Church St.

Kaufman Lake

Eisner Park

University Ave.

Springfield Ave.

John St,

Mattis Ave.

Russell Ave.

John St,

Kenwood Dr.

Centennial Park

Clark Park
150

Hessel Park

Mayfair Park

Kirby Ave.

Roby Recreational Trail

Boulware Trail

Broadmor

Robeson Park
P

Mayfair

Devonshire Dr.

57

Duncan Rd.

Robert P. Simon Trail

Windsor Rd.

Harrington

Morrisey Park

Galen

Mattis Park

Continues to Mattis
1 miles west of Duncan

Noel Park

Galen

University of Illinois

MILE SCALE

0   1   2

57

10

Hogan St.

Match Line

Location & Setting	The cities of Champaign and Urbana in east central Illinois. The paths generally parallel streets or through parks. The setting is urban and is the home of the University of Illinois.
Information	Champaign County Regional Planning Commission 1303 N. Cunningham Road /P.O. Box 339 Urbana, IL 61801 (217) 328-3313
County	Champaign

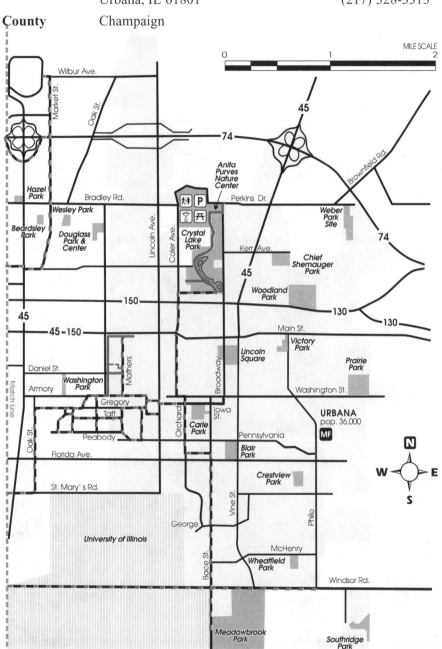

Champaign County

Chicago Lakefront Bike Path

Trail Length	Approximately 20 miles
Surface	Paved
Uses	Leisure bicycling, in-line skating, jogging

Northern Section

Parking, accesses, restrooms, water, and refreshments located throughout the bikeway.

N
W — E
S

NORTH BRANCH TO LAKEFRONT BIKE PATH CONNECTION

MATCH LINE

MILE SCALE

0   1   2   3

FACILITIES

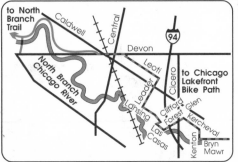

🔧 Bike Repair

Location & Setting	From the north, the bike path begins around Bryn Mawr (5600 north) and Sheridan Road, then proceeds south along the shoreline of Lake Michigan to 71st Street. Urban lakefront.
Information	Bureau of Traffic, Engineering and Operations 320 N. Clark Street Chicago, IL 60610
County	Cook　　　　　Chicago pop. 3,000,000

Southern Section

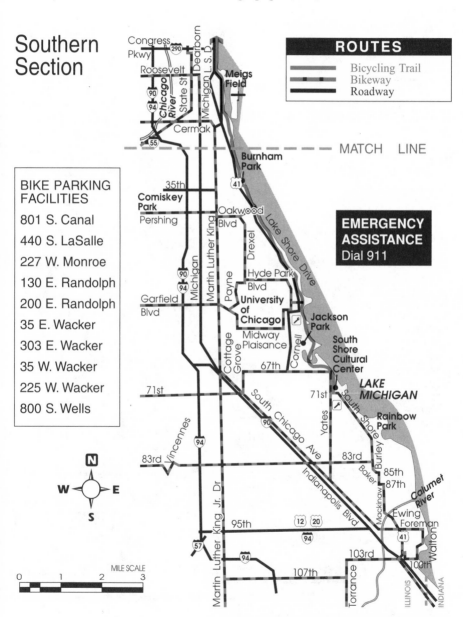

ROUTES

Bicycling Trail
Bikeway
Roadway

MATCH LINE

EMERGENCY ASSISTANCE
Dial 911

BIKE PARKING FACILITIES

801 S. Canal
440 S. LaSalle
227 W. Monroe
130 E. Randolph
200 E. Randolph
35 E. Wacker
303 E. Wacker
35 W. Wacker
225 W. Wacker
800 S. Wells

Chicago Lakefront Bike Path

Churchill Woods Forest Preserve

Trail Length	3.8 miles
Surface	Screenings, mowed turf
Uses	Leisure and fat tire bicycling, cross country skiing, hiking/jogging
Location & Setting	The 259 acre preserve is located between Lombard and Glen Ellyn in north central DuPage County. Setting is woodlands, prairie and river.
Information	Forest Preserve District of DuPage County (630) 790-4900 185 Spring Avenue Glen Ellyn, IL 60138
County	DuPage

Picnicking is popular and camping facilities are available.

The east branch of the DuPage River provides more than two miles of waterway frontage.

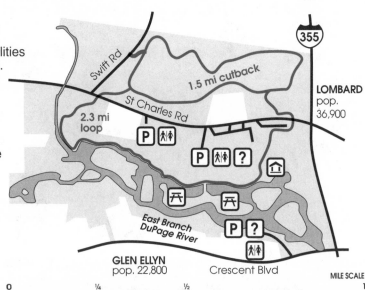

Churchill Wood Forest Preserve offers one of the last native prairies in DuPage County.

Comlara Park

Trail Length	10.5 miles
Surface	Natural turf
Uses	Fat tire bicycling (easy to difficult), hiking
Location & Setting	Located in north central Illinois approximately 12 miles north of Bloomington/Normal. The several trails encompass Evergreen Lake. Setting is wooded with lakefront and hills.
Information	McLean County Parks and Recreation (309) 726-2022 Comlara Park—R.R. #1 Box 73 Hudson, IL 61746
County	McLean

No water or restrooms are available on these trails.

From Visitor Center to:

Hwy. 51 .... 2 miles

Normal/Bloomington .. 12 miles

Trails are restricted to single file, are natural turf surface, and are continually changing and variable.

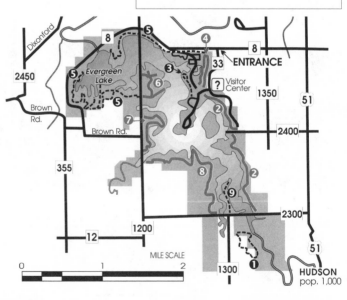

No.	Trail Name	Miles	Effort Level
1.	Shady Hollow Nature Trail *	1.00	Easy
2.	Deer Island Area Access Trail	2.50	Difficult
3.	Hickory Grove Nature Trail *	.50	Easy
4.	Campers Park Access Trail	1.50	Moderate
5.	Lakeview Area Access Trail	3.00	Moderate
6.	White Oak Area Access Trail	.50	Easy
7.	Two Cedars Prairie Access Trail	.50	Easy
8.	Southern Zone Access Trail	2.50	Moderate
9.	Mallard Cove Access Trail *	.25	Moderate

* Foot traffic only

Constitution Trail

Trail Length	5.2 miles
Surface	Paved asphalt
Uses	Leisure bicycling, in-line skating, cross country skiing, jogging
Location & Setting	Located in Bloomington & Normal beginning at Jefferson & Robinson Streets to Airport Road.
Information	McLean County Chamber of Commerce (309) 829-1641 210 South East Street • Bloomington, IL 61702
	McLean County Wheelers Bicycle Club (309) 454-1541
	Friends of the Constitution Trail P.O. Box 4494 • Bloomington, IL 61702
	Bloomington Parks & Recreation Dept. (309) 823-4260 109 East Olive Street • Bloomington, IL 61701

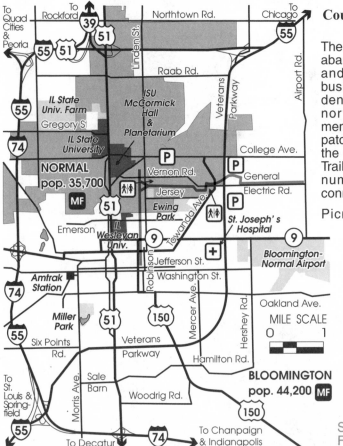

County   McClean

The trail is built on an abandoned trail bed and runs through business and residential areas. The north/south segment is wooded with patches of prairie on the eastern section. Trail accesses from numerous street connections.

Picnic tables and benches are located along the trail. Both Illinois State University and Wesleyan University are located within a short distance of the trail.

Open from dawn to dusk.

SEE PAGE 77 FOR LEGENDS

Crystal Lake Trails

	● Prairie Trail	● Sterne's Woods	● Veteran Acres	W. Herrick Lippold Pk.	Winding Creek
Trail Length	7 mi.	2.1 mi.	7.5 mi.	3.5 mi.	2.5 mi.
Surface	pvd./scrn'g	paved/dirt road	paved/natural	screenings	paved
Uses*	L, H	F, H, X	F, H, X	L, H	L, S

Location & Setting	These trails are located throughout the Crystal Lake area. McHenry County is a favorite destination for water sport activities by Chicagoland residents.
Information	Crystal Lake Park District (815) 459-0680 One East Crystal Lake Avenue Crystal Lake, IL 60014
County	McHenry ● See Detail Maps

---

* USES
L = Leisure Bicycling
F = Fat Tire Bicycling
S = in-line skating
H = Hiking, Jogging
X = Cross country skiing

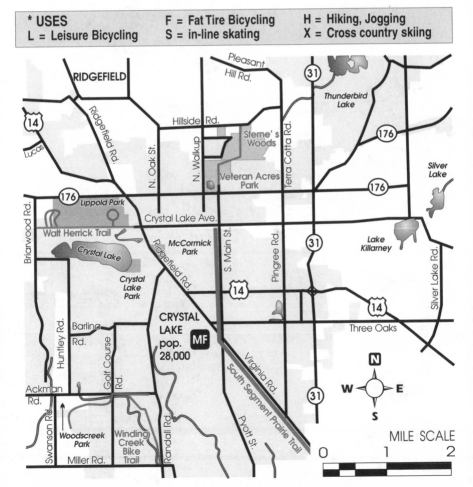

Danada Forest Preserve

Trail Length	2.0 miles of bicycling trails, 2.9 miles total
Surface	Limestone screenings
Uses	Leisure bicycling, cross country skiing, hiking jogging, horseback riding
Location & Setting	Danada Forest Preserve located in the city of Wheaton in central DuPage County, can be accessed from Naperville Road, ½ mile north of Interstate 88. Prairie, woodland, and marsh.
Information	Forest Preserve District of DuPage County (630) 790-4900 185 Spring Avenue Glen Ellyn, IL 60138
	Danada Forest Preserve (630) 668-6012
County	DuPage

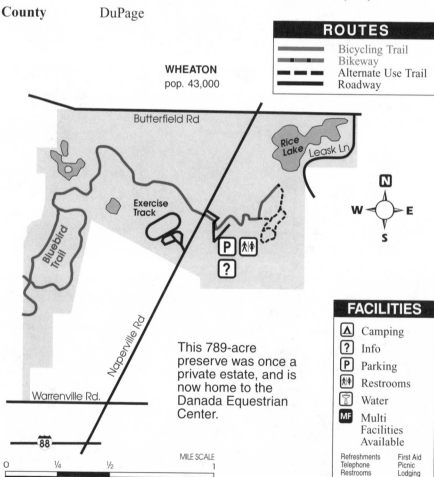

WHEATON
pop. 43,000

ROUTES

- Bicycling Trail
- Bikeway
- Alternate Use Trail
- Roadway

Butterfield Rd

Rice Lake

Leask Ln

Exercise Track

Bluebird Trail

Naperville Rd

Warrenville Rd.

88

This 789-acre preserve was once a private estate, and is now home to the Danada Equestrian Center.

N
W — E
S

FACILITIES

A	Camping
?	Info
P	Parking
♦♦	Restrooms
⍦	Water
MF	Multi Facilities Available

Refreshments   First Aid
Telephone   Picnic
Restrooms   Lodging

MILE SCALE

0   ¼   ½   1

Deer Grove Bicycle Trail

Trail Length	4.0 miles
Surface	Paved
Uses	Leisure bicycling, x-c skiing, jogging/hiking
Location & Setting	The Deer Grove Preserve consists of rolling upland forest interspersed with wooded ravines and wetlands. Creeks meander through the tract, feeding two lakes located in the preserve. Open spaces, wooded areas (connects to Palatine Trail).
Information	Forest Preserve District of Cook County (708) 366-9420 536 N. Harlem Avenue River Forest, IL 60305
County	Cook

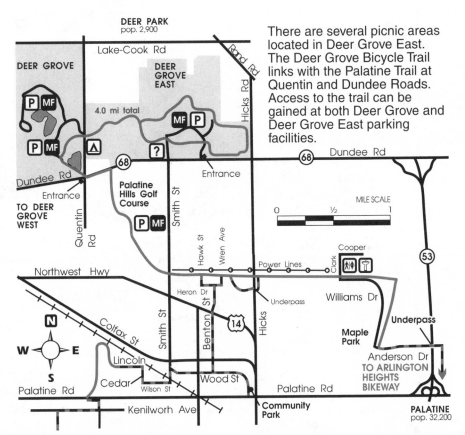

There are several picnic areas located in Deer Grove East. The Deer Grove Bicycle Trail links with the Palatine Trail at Quentin and Dundee Roads. Access to the trail can be gained at both Deer Grove and Deer Grove East parking facilities.

You can ride through a mature forest past a herd of elk, then head for the lake to watch the sailboats. There are six fishing walls if you are inclined to do some fishing along with your bicycling.

Delyte Morris Bicycle Way

Trail Length	5 miles (2.6 path and 2.4 streets)
Surface	Paved and crushed stone
Uses	Leisure bicycling, hiking
Location & Setting	This bicycle way goes from the courthouse in Edwardsville to Bluff Road on the western edge of the Southern Illinois University campus. From Edwardsville the trail proceeds down a small valley and through some heavily wooded area. Sections are rugged with hilly terrain. Once out of the woods, it follows an old railroad right-of-way, through prairie areas and the grade is easy.
Information	Campus Recreation (618) 692-3235 Southern Illinois University Edwardsville, IL 62026
County	Madison

FACILITIES

P Parking

MF Multi Facilities Available

Refreshments   First Aid
Telephone   Picnic
Restrooms   Lodging

ROUTES

Bicycling Trail
Bikeway
Roadway

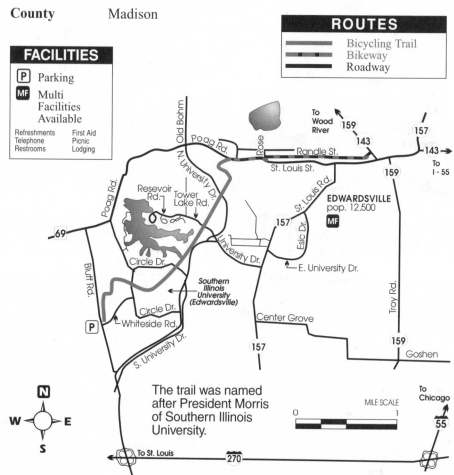

The trail was named after President Morris of Southern Illinois University.

— 44 —

Illinois Plants

In spring, nearly every wooded park in the state seems to burst with wildflowers. Some of the best bets are Mississippi Palisades near Savanna, Starved Rock near Ottawa, Pere Marquette near Grafton, and Giant City near Carbondale. Starved Rock has an annual wildflower pilgrimage during the first weekend in May.

Prairie wildflowers are best from June through September Illinois Beach State Park at Zion is one of the better places to find wildflowers. Goose Lake Prairie, near Morris, and Pere Marquette State Park are also good areas. Interpreters are available year-round at these sites.

The White Oak, Illinois' state tree

Sand Ridge State Forest, about 25 miles southwest of Peoria, is the largest state forest, encompassing 7,500 acres. More than half of the area is covered by native oak and hickory. The white oak, the state tree, can reach a height of 80 feet. When young, it has a pyramid shape; as it matures, it becomes broadly rounded.

The White Oak leaf with acorns

In 1818, 23 percent of Illinois was covered with wetlands. Today, wetlands account for only 2.6 percent of the state. These important ecological zones are habitats for many kinds of trees and plant life. The bald cypress grows only in swamps and bottomland forests, such as at Heron Pond and Long Reach, both located in the Cache River State Natural Area of southern Illinois.

The Kankakee mallow is an herb that resembles the holly-hock, standing about five feet tall. Its blue flowers contain five petals. Its fruit resembles little round cheeses cut into segments. The plant is found only on Langham Island in the Kankakee River.

The small whorled pogonia is a small orchid, with greenish one-inch-long flowers that grow only in a wooded preserve of southern Illinois. The federal government has listed it as endangered throughout its range.

The mountain clematis is a woody vine that flaunts blue-to-purple flowers in May and June. In Illinois, the plant's habitat is isolated and unusual, it grows only on algific slopes (north-facing rocky slopes that retain cold air throughout the year).

Des Plaines Division

Trail Length	12 miles
Surface	Natural groomed (5 to 10 feet wide)
Uses	Fat tire bicycling, hiking, horseback riding
Location & Setting	Located along the east bank of the Des Plaines River in northwest Cook County. It begins at Touhy Avenue, east of Mannheim Road, and continues north to the Lake-Cook County line. The setting is river bottom with woods, open areas and small hills.

Information Emergency Assistance   911

Cook County Forest Preserve District   (847) 366-9420
536 North Harlem Avenue
River Forest, IL 60305

County Cook

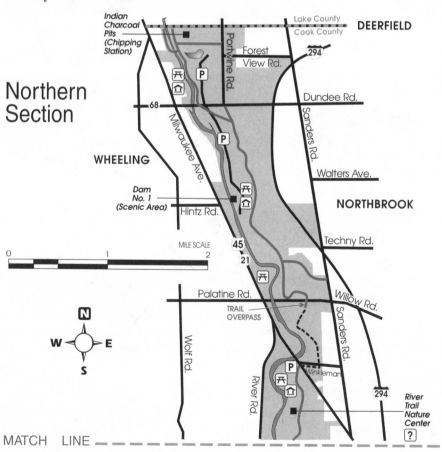

Northern
Section

ROUTES

![bicycling]	Bicycling Trail
- - -	Alternate Use Trail
![roadway]	Roadway

FACILITIES

+	First Aid
?	Info
P	Parking
🎑	Picnic
🏠	Shelter

Southern Section

MILE SCALE
0   1   2

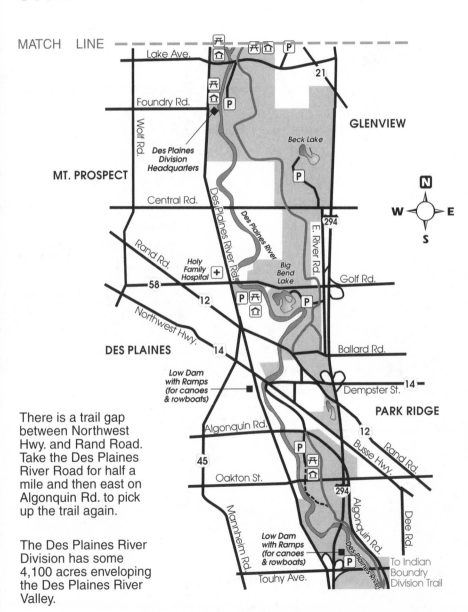

MATCH LINE

Lake Ave.

Foundry Rd.

Wolf Rd.

GLENVIEW

Beck Lake

Des Plaines Division Headquarters

MT. PROSPECT

Central Rd.

Des Plaines River Rd.

Des Plaines River

E. River Rd.

294

21

N
W ⟶ E
S

Rand Rd.

Holy Family Hospital +

58

Big Bend Lake

Golf Rd.

12

Northwest Hwy.

DES PLAINES

14

Low Dam with Ramps (for canoes & rowboats)

Ballard Rd.

Dempster St.

14

PARK RIDGE

There is a trail gap between Northwest Hwy. and Rand Road. Take the Des Plaines River Road for half a mile and then east on Algonquin Rd. to pick up the trail again.

The Des Plaines River Division has some 4,100 acres enveloping the Des Plaines River Valley.

Algonquin Rd.

45

Oakton St.

Mannheim Rd.

12

Busse Hwy.

Rand Rd.

294

Dee Rd.

Algonquin Rd.

Low Dam with Ramps (for canoes & rowboats)

P

Touhy Ave.

Des Plaines River

To Indian Boundry Division Trail

Des Plaines Division

Des Plaines River Trail

Trail Length	33 miles (49.0 with loops)
Surface	Limestone screenings
Uses	Leisure bicycling, cross country skiing, hiking, horseback riding (Snowmobiling in northern section only)
Location & Setting	The Des Plaines River Trail parallels its namesake river through Lake County. Open area such as prairies and savannas are common. As you travel through this river valley, look for changes in the landscape. In northern Lake County, the valley is wide and the river meanders. In southern Lake County, the valley is narrow and the river runs a straighter course. Woodlands are more common.
Information	Lake County Forest Preserves (847) 367-6640 2000 N. Milwaukee Avenue Libertyville, IL 60048
County	Lake

Van Patten Woods consists of 972 acres. Enjoy picnic areas, reserveable shelters and shoreline fishing at 74 acre Sterling Lake.

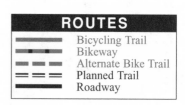

ROUTES	
▬▬▬	Bicycling Trail
▬ ▬ ▬	Bikeway
▬ ▬ ▬	Alternate Bike Trail
≡ ≡ ≡	Planned Trail
▬▬▬	Roadway

LAKE COUNTY FOREST PRESERVES

Open daily from 8 am to sunset daily. Alcoholic beverages may not be consumed in or near parking areas. Pets are permitted, except in picnic areas, but must be controlled on a leash (no longer than 10 feet). Forest Preserve Ranger Police regularly patrol the Preserves. Ranger Police receive the same basic training as other Illinois police officers and have the same authority.

More than 18,500 acres make up the Lake County Forest Preserves, a dynamic and unique system of natural and cultural resources.

FACILITIES	
[?]	Info
[P]	Parking
[⊼]	Picnic
[⑪]	Refreshments
[⋔]	Restrooms
[⌂]	Shelter
[🛉]	Water

The southern end of the Des Plaines River Trail currently ends at Hwy. 45 in the Half Day Forest Preserve. Across the river is Wright Woods Forest Preserve. Moving north, the trail passes through MacArthur Woods Forest Preserve in Mettawa and ends at Old School Forest Preserve in Libertyville.

Northern Section

Southern Section

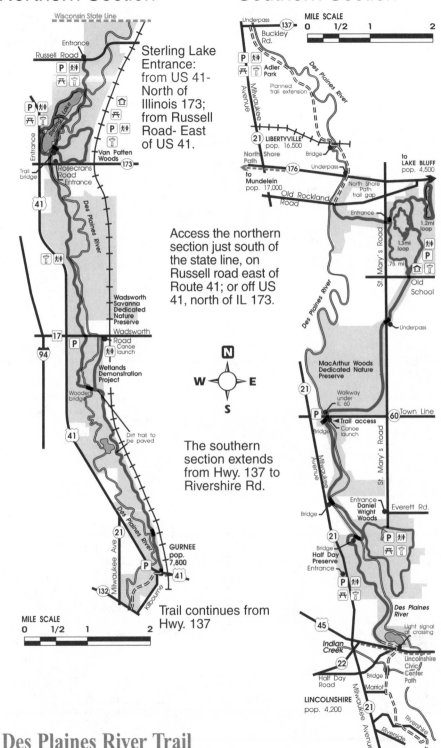

Northern Section labels:

Wisconsin State Line

Entrance
Russell Road

Sterling Lake

Entrance

Trail bridge

Rosecrans Road Entrance

Van Patten Woods

41

173

Des Plaines River

Wadsworth Savanna Dedicated Nature Preserve

Wadsworth Road
Canoe launch

17
94

Wetlands Demonstration Project

Wooden bridge

Dirt trail to be paved

41

Des Plaines River

21

GURNEE pop. 7,800

P

41

Milwaukee Ave

132

Kilbourne

Sterling Lake Entrance: from US 41- North of Illinois 173; from Russell Road- East of US 41.

Access the northern section just south of the state line, on Russell road east of Route 41; or off US 41, north of IL 173.

The southern section extends from Hwy. 137 to Rivershire Rd.

Compass: N W E S

Trail continues from Hwy. 137

Southern Section labels:

MILE SCALE 0 1/2 1 2

Underpass
137
Buckley Rd.

Adler Park

Des Plaines River

Planned trail extension

Milwaukee Avenue

21 LIBERTYVILLE pop. 16,500

Bridge

North Shore Path

176 Underpass

to Mundelein pop. 17,000

Old Rockland Road

North Shore Path trail gap

to LAKE BLUFF pop. 4,500

1.2mi loop

1.3mi loop

.75 mi

St. Mary's Road

Old School

Entrance

Underpass

MacArthur Woods Dedicated Nature Preserve

21

Walkway under IL 60

60 Town Line

P Trail access
Canoe launch

Bridge

Milwaukee Avenue

St. Mary's Road

Entrance Daniel Wright Woods

Everett Rd.

P

Bridge

21

Bridge

Half Day Preserve Entrance

P

Des Plaines River

Light signal at crossing

45

Indian Creek

22

Half Day Road

LINCOLNSHIRE pop. 4,200

Marriot

Lincolnshire Civic Center Path

Bridge

Milwaukee Avenue

21

Riverside

Rivershire

MILE SCALE 0 1/2 1 2

Des Plaines River Trail

Evanston Bike Paths/ North Shore Channel

Trail Length	7.0 miles
Surface	Paved
Uses	Leisure bicycling, in-line skating, jogging
Location & Setting	City of Evanston in northeast Cook County north of Chicago and bordering Lake Michigan. Setting is urban, North Shore Channel is open park area.
Information	Evanston Chamber of Commerce (847) 328-1510 807 Davis Street Evanston, IL 60201
County	Cook

**EVANSTON-
LAKE SHORE
PATH TO
GREEN BAY
TRAIL**

Lincoln St.
west to
Ashland
(1 mi.)

Ashland north
to Isabella
(.4 mi.)

Isabella west
to Poplar Dr.
(.4 mi.)

Poplar Dr.
north to Forest
Ave.
(1 mi.)

**EMERGENCY
ASSISTANCE**

Dial 911

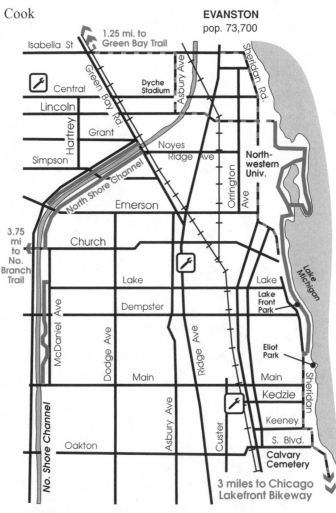

Fermilab Bike Trail

Trail Length	4.0 miles
Surface	Paved
Uses	Leisure bicycling, cross country skiing, hiking
Location & Setting	The east access is off Batavia Road just west of Hwy. 59. The west access is off Kirk Road about ¾ miles north of Butterfield Road. Tall grass prairie, flood plain woods and wetlands.
Information	Fermilab Prairie Path Volunteers (630) 840-3351
County	DuPage

You can learn about everything from subatomic particles to bison at Fermilab. Built in the 1950's, Fermilab is on the cutting edge of particle acceleration research. However, don't miss the woods, ponds, and prairie. The top floor (15th) is open for observation, and can provide a spectacular view of the Fox Valley.

As an alternate, tour the scenic 4 mile trail through Fermilab, or extend it to a 14 mile round trip by way of the Aurora Branch, Batavia Spur and paved paths along Kirk Road and Batavia Road.

FACILITIES

🛠	Bike Repair
P	Parking
🚻	Restrooms
MF	Multi Facilities Available

Refreshments	First Aid
Telephone	Picnic
Restrooms	Lodging

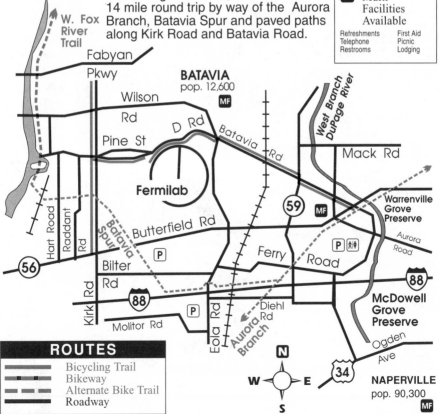

ROUTES
- Bicycling Trail
- Bikeway
- Alternate Bike Trail
- Roadway

Fox River Trail

Trail Length	41.7 miles
Surface	Paved, limestone screenings
Uses	Leisure bicycling, cross country skiing, hiking
Location & Setting	Follows the Fox River between Crystal Lake and Aurora. Open spaces and small communities.
Information	Fox Valley Park District (630) 897-0516 P.O. Box 808 Aurora, IL 60507
	Dundee Township Tourist Center (847) 426-2255 319 N. River Road East Dundee, IL 60118
County	McHenry, Kane

This trail winds through the Fox River Valley running northward from Aurora to Crystal Lake. You'll bike through forest and nature preserves, and several historic and interesting communities. This popular trail connects to the Illinois Prairie Path to the east, to the Great Western Trail west of St. Charles and to the Virgil Gilman Trail in Aurora. Plans include extending the trail via bikeways through Crystal Lake, then connecting to the Prairie Trail (north section) which will continue to the Wisconsin state line.

Red Oak Nature Center is a 40 acre oak and maple forest on the east bank of the Fox River. Inside the nature center building, you'll find a contemporary museum stressing the four basic elements of life...sun, air, water and soil.

ROUTES

▬▬▬	Bicycling Trail
▬ ▬ ▬	Alternate Bike Trail
▬▬▬	Roadway

Devil's Cave is one of the most unusual natural features on the trail. Although small, this is one of the very few caves in northeastern Illinois. Rich in folklore, this cave is believed to have been used by the Pottawatomie Indians.

ROUTE SLIP	SEGMENT	TOTAL
Crystal Lk. Rd.(Crystal Lake)		
Hwy. 62 (Algonquin)	4.0	41.7
Bolz Rd. (Carpentersville)	3.0	37.7
Hwy. 72/68 (E. Dundee)	4.0	34.7
Hwy. 90 (Elgin)	3.5	30.7
Hwy. 20 (Elgin)	5.1	27.2
River Crossing (S. Elgin)	2.9	22.1
Black Hawk Forest Pres.	2.2	19.2
Army Trail Rd. (St. Chas.)	2.5	17.0
Main St. (St. Charles)	3.0	14.5
State St. (Geneva)	2.0	11.5
Fabyan Pkwy. (Batavia)	1.5	9.5
Wilson St. (Batavia)	1.0	8.0
Hwy. 88	5.0	7.0
New York St. (Aurora)	2.0	2.0

FACILITIES

🔧	Bike Repair
➕	First Aid
❓	Info
🛏	Lodging
P	Parking
🪑	Picnic
🍴	Refreshments
🚻	Restrooms
🏠	Shelter
MF	Multi Facilities Available

Refreshments   First Aid
Telephone   Picnic
Restrooms   Lodging

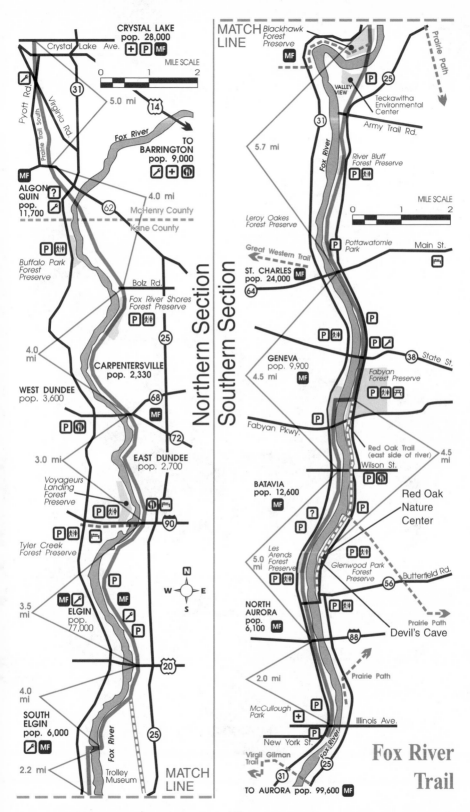

CRYSTAL LAKE
pop. 28,000

Crystal Lake Ave.

MILE SCALE
0 1 2

5.0 mi

Fox River

TO BARRINGTON
pop. 9,000

Pyott Rd.

Virginia Rd.

Prairie Trail South

31

14

ALGON QUIN
pop. 11,700

4.0 mi

McHenry County

Kane County

62

Buffalo Park Forest Preserve

Bolz Rd.

Fox River Shores Forest Preserve

25

4.0 mi

CARPENTERSVILLE
pop. 2,330

WEST DUNDEE
pop. 3,600

68

72

3.0 mi

EAST DUNDEE
pop. 2,700

Voyageurs Landing Forest Preserve

90

Tyler Creek Forest Preserve

3.5 mi

ELGIN
pop. 77,000

20

4.0 mi

SOUTH ELGIN
pop. 6,000

Fox River

2.2 mi

Trolley Museum

25

Northern Section

Southern Section

MATCH LINE

MATCH LINE

Blackhawk Forest Preserve

MF

VALLEY VIEW

25

31

Teckawitha Environmental Center

Army Trail Rd.

5.7 mi

River Bluff Forest Preserve

Leroy Oakes Forest Preserve

MILE SCALE
0 1 2

Great Western Trail

Pottawatomie Park

Main St.

ST. CHARLES
pop. 24,000

64

38 State St.

GENEVA
pop. 9,900

4.5 mi

Fabyan Forest Preserve

Fabyan Pkwy.

Red Oak Trail (east side of river)

4.5 mi

Wilson St.

BATAVIA
pop. 12,600

Red Oak Nature Center

Les Arends Forest Preserve

5.0 mi

Glenwood Park Forest Preserve

56 Butterfield Rd.

Prairie Path

NORTH AURORA
pop. 6,100

88

Devil's Cave

2.0 mi

Prairie Path

McCullough Park

Illinois Ave.

New York St.

Virgil Gilman Trail

31

25

TO AURORA pop. 99,600

Fox River Trail

Prairie Path

N
W   E
S

Fullersburg Forest Preserve

Trail Length	2.5 miles of bicycling trails, 3.25 miles total
Surface	Screenings, Asphalt
Uses	Leisure bicycling, cross country skiing, hiking/jogging, horseback riding
Location & Setting	Located between Oak Brook and Hinsdale in east central DuPage County, Fullersburg Forest Preserve can be accessed from Spring Road, ½ mile northwest of York Road. Woodlands, prairie, creek.
Information	Forest Preserve District of DuPage County (630) 790-4900 185 Spring Avenue Glen Ellyn, IL 60138
County	Du Page

Fullersburg Woods, with 221 acres, is a nature sanctuary for plants and animals. It has a Visitors and Environmental Center which is open daily from 9am to 5pm.

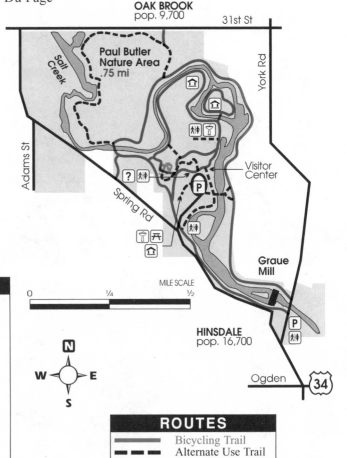

FACILITIES

- ✚ First Aid
- ? Info
- P Parking
- 🎪 Picnic
- 🚻 Restrooms
- 🏠 Shelter
- 🚰 Water
- **MF** Multi Facilities Available

Refreshments   First Aid
Telephone   Picnic
Restrooms   Lodging

ROUTES

▬▬▬	Bicycling Trail
▬ ▬ ▬	Alternate Use Trail
═══	Planned Trail
▬▬▬	Roadway

Fulton Bike Trail (F.A.S.T.)

Trail Length	6 miles existing, 8+ miles planned
Surface	Asphalt, shared streets
Uses	Leisure bicycling, in-line skating, cross country skiing, hiking
Location & Setting	Located in Fulton along the Mississippi River in northwest Illinois. Setting is riverfront, city streets.
Information	Fulton Chamber of Commerce P.O. Box 253 Fulton, IL 61252
County	Whiteside

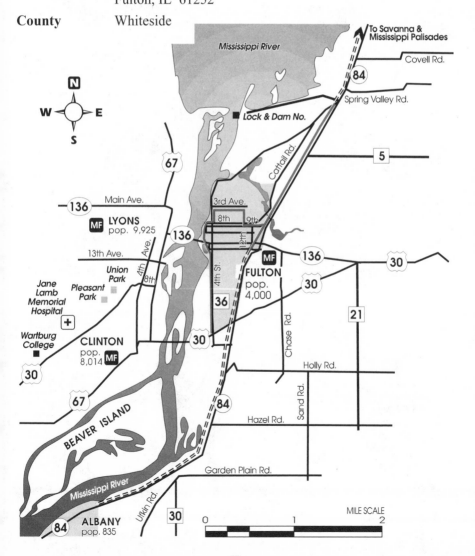

Grand Illinois Trail

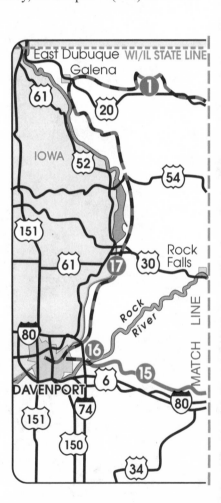

Trail Length	475 miles
Location & Setting	Existing and planned trails forming a loop of northern Illinois, from the suburbs of Chicago to the Mississippi and from the Wisconsin border to the I & M Canal.
Information	Illinois Department of Conservation (217) 782-3715 Office of Public Information 524 South Second Street Springfield, IL 62701-1787
	Rails-to-Trails Conservancy, IL Chapter (217) 789-4782 319 West Cook Street Springfield, IL 62704
County	Covers 16 counties

A series of 17 trails and road segments covering several hundred miles looping Northern Illinois. Some of the proposed route is still conceptual, with linkages to trails via lightly traveled roads and streets.

ROUTES

▬▬▬	Bicycling Trail
▬ ▬ ▬	Bikeway
▬▬▬	Roadway

GRAND ILLINOIS TRAIL SYSTEM SEGMENTS

1. Local roads
2. Pecatonica Trail
3. Rockford Area Trails
4. Stone Bridge and Long Prairie Trails
5. Conceptual connection
6. Crystal Lake/Harvard Trail segment
7. Prairie Trail segment
8. Fox River Trail segment
9. Illinois Prairie Path segment
10. Des Plaines River Trail segment
11. Centennial Trail
12. Lockport Historical & Joliet Heritage Trails (& roads)
13. Illinois and Michigan (I & M) Canal State Trail segment
14. Conceptual connection
15. Hennepin Canal State Trail segment
16. Conceptual connection
17. Great River Trail

Grand Illinois Trail

Grant Woods Forest Preserve

Trail Length	3.3 miles
Surface	Limestone screenings
Uses	Leisure bicycling, cross country skiing, jogging, snowmobiling
Location & Setting	Grant Woods is east of Fox Lake and bounded by Rte. 59 on the west, Rte. 83 on the east, Rte. 132 north and Rte. 134 south. Enter on Monaville Rd. east of Rte. 59. The northern half is largely marsh and prairie.
Information	Lake County Forest Preserve (847) 367-6640 2000 N. Milwaukee Avenue Libertyville, IL 60043
County	Lake

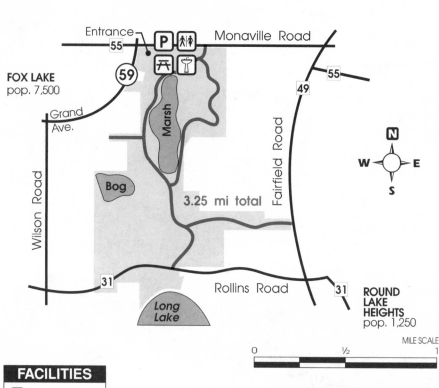

Mammals

The white-tailed deer, the largest Illinois mammal, is one of the state's most prevalent mammals. The deer eats twigs, shrubs, grasses, and acorns. It snorts when alarmed and, when on the run, can jump more than 8 feet vertically or 30 feet horizontally.

Birds

The great horned owl is the only large owl in North America with ear tufts and is one of the state's most common owls. It has a heavily barred belly and a white collar or bib. Listen for its resonant call: "who-whoooo-whooo." The nocturnal bird relies on keen eyesight and hearing to hunt. The female lays eggs in February, and because they must be protected from freezing, you may see her covered with snow while sitting on the nest.

Illinois is in the path of the Mississippi Flyway, the migration route used by waterfowl through 14 Midwestern states. More than 1.1 million ducks and geese winter in Illinois every year. Important wintering areas are Horseshoe Lake Conservation Area, Union County Refuge Area, and Rend Lake. Goose Lake Prairie State Natural Area, 60 miles southwest of Chicago, not only contains the largest native prairie in Illinois but more than half of it is a dedicated nature preserve. Wild ducks and geese concentrate in its marshlands in spring and fall.

The mallard duck is a common waterfowl that loves freshwater lakes, ponds, sloughs, and reservoirs. It will build its nest on the ground, concealed in tall grass. The Canada goose has a brown-gray back, a long black neck, and a distinct white chin strap. Its call is a haunting "ka-ronk."

Great River Trail
Ben Butterworth Pathway

Trail Length	62.0 miles
Surface	Paved paths (10 feet), shared streets, undeveloped
Uses	Leisure bicycling, in-line skating, cross country skiing, hiking/jogging
Location & Setting	The Great River Trail runs from Rock Island to the Mississippi Palisades State Park, north of Savanna, along the Mississippi River in northwest Illinois. The setting is riverfront, urban to small communities, rural, woods, open areas, farmland.
Information	Bi-State Regional Commission — (309) 793-6300 1504 Third Avenue / P.O. Box 3365 Rock Island, IL 61204
	Parks & Recreation Dept. — (309) 752-1573 1400 Tenth Street East Moline, IL 61244
	Hampton Village Hall — (309) 755-7165 520 First Avenue Hampton, IL 61256
County	Rock Island, Whiteside, Carroll

FACILITIES

- ➕ First Aid
- 🛏 Lodging
- P Parking
- 🍴 Refreshments
- MF Multi Facilities Available

Refreshments   First Aid
Telephone   Picnic
Restrooms   Lodging

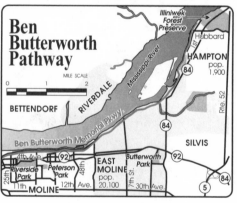

There are undeveloped gaps throughout its length, especially north of Hampton.

Trailheads

Rock Island	Sunset Park, 18th Avenue and IL Route 92
East Moline	Waterfront & Mississippi Parks (north sides of city)
Hampton	Riverfront Park (south side), Illiniwek Park (north side)
Rapids City	Shuler's Shady Grove Park
Port Byron	Boat access area
Albany	Boat access area
Thomson	Downtown area, Thomson Causeway, Buck's Barn
Savanna	Downtown area

Mississippi Palisades State Park

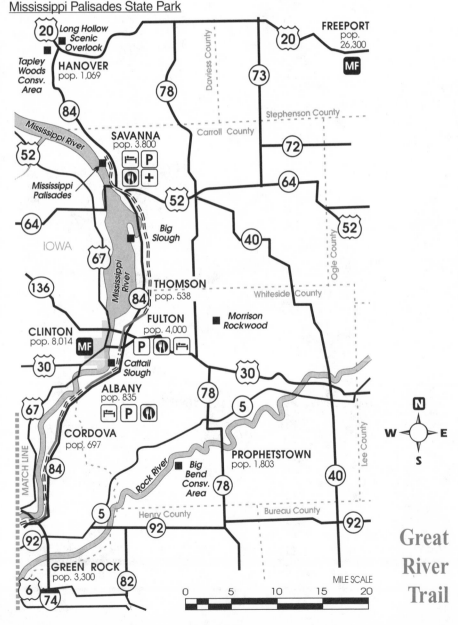

ROUTES

Bicycling Trail
Planned Trail
Roadway

Great
River
Trail

Great Western Trail

Trail Length	18 miles
Surface	Limestone screenings
Uses	Leisure bicycling, cross country skiing, hiking/ jogging, snowmobiling
Location & Setting	This 18 mile trail extends from the LeRoy Oakes Forest Preserve west of St. Charles to Sycamore at Old State and Airport Road in Kane and DeKalb counties and stands on the former site of the Chicago and Northwestern Railroad line. Rural landscape, wetlands, farmlands, small communities.
Information	Kane County Forest Preserve (630) 232-5980 719 Batavia Avenue, Building G Geneva, IL 60134
County	DeKalb, Kane

There is a bike route from the city of DeKalb to a nature trail. The Peace Road Trail links DeKalb and Sycamore with a recreational path.

SYCAMORE pop. 9,200

VIRGIL

LILY LAKE

I.C. Trail

Empire Rd.

LeRoy Oakes Forest Preserve

to Fox River Trail

Campton Forest Preserve

WASCO

Compton Hills Dr.

ST. CHARLES pop. 24,000

MILE SCALE
0 1 2 3 4 5

ROUTES		FACILITIES	
▬▬	Bicycling Trail	🔧	Bike Repair
▬▬	Roadway	?	Info

FACILITIES

- 🔧 Bike Repair
- ? Info
- 🛏 Lodging
- P Parking
- 🛋 Picnic
- 🍴 Refreshments
- 🚻 Restrooms
- MF Multi Facilities Available

Refreshments   First Aid
 Telephone   Picnic
 Restrooms   Lodging

N
 W — E
 S

There are plans to provide a 3.5 mile corridor between the Fox River Trail and the Great Western Trail. The path will run south from Silver Glen Road along Randall Road on a county highway easement to LeRoy Oakes Forest Preserve, where it will connect with the Great Western Trail.

The Great Western Trail is a rail-to-trails conversion. Horseback riding is permitted from Lily Lake to LeRoy Oakes. Snowmobiling is permitted with 4 or more inches of snow.

Reptiles and Amphibians in Illinois

THE BIRD-VOICED TREE FROG—This unusual animal is found mainly in the extreme southern parts of the state. The small, smooth-skinned frog is gray and green in color and usually has an asymmetrical star-shaped dark blotch on its back. It is named for the long, quivering birdlike note the male frog makes when it calls for a mate during summer. It breeds on stems and branches above water.

The Illinois chorus frog is found near ponds in the sand prairie. This little frog breeds during March. The male's call sounds like a series of short, loud, birdlike whistles. The frog is a dull gray color with light brown markings on its back. The largest specimen is 1.6 inches long (not including its legs). The Illinois chorus frog is listed as a threatened species.

The endangered western hognose snake has an upturned snout that looks like a pig's nose. It is a medium-size, stout-bodied snake. Its belly and the underside of its tail are predominantly black. Its back is gray-tan with brown blotches. It spends much of its time looking for toads, birds, and mice. This snake is not venomous.

Illinois State Fish — Bluegill

The bluegill (*Lepomis macrochirus*) is a very common fish throughout the state. It is most abundant in clear lakes with large amounts of aquatic vegetation. However, it occurs in a large variety of habitats including pools, overflow ponds, oxbows, swamps, and man-made impoundments. They often occur in small loose schools that have up to 20 to 30 individuals in them.

They are generally small to medium-sized fish. The largest one reported from Illinois weighed 1.6 kilograms (3 lb. 8oz.). More typically, one would weigh about 0.3 kilograms (12 oz.) and would be about 24 centimeters (9.5 in.) long.

Bluegills are generally carnivorous. They mainly eat aquatic insects and insect larvae; in addition, they eat smaller fish, crayfish, and snails. When other food is in short supply, they will also eat algae.

In the summer male bluegills build nests in water less than about 60 centimeters (2 ft.) deep. These nests are shallow, circular depressions and are frequently in areas with gravel bottoms. Often many males build nests in a small area. Females lay eggs in the nests. The males then guard the eggs until they hatch.

Green Bay Trail

Trail Length	16.3 miles
Surface	Paved
Uses	Leisure bicycling, cross country skiing, hiking
Location & Setting	From Wilmette in northeast Cook County to Lake Bluff in southeast Lake County and primarily along the Chicago and Northwestern rail line. Urban setting.
Information	Lake County Dept. of Transportation (847) 362-3950 600 W. Winchester Road Libertyville, IL 60048
County	Cook, Lake

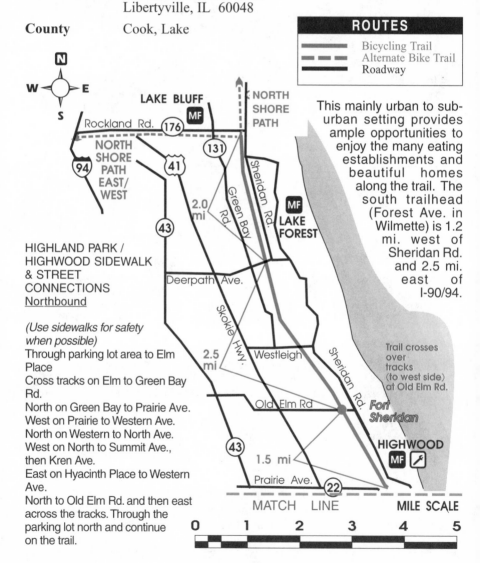

ROUTES

Bicycling Trail
Alternate Bike Trail
Roadway

This mainly urban to sub-urban setting provides ample opportunities to enjoy the many eating establishments and beautiful homes along the trail. The south trailhead (Forest Ave. in Wilmette) is 1.2 mi. west of Sheridan Rd. and 2.5 mi. east of I-90/94.

LAKE BLUFF
NORTH SHORE PATH
Rockland Rd. 176
NORTH SHORE PATH EAST/WEST
94
41
131
43
Sheridan Rd.
Green Bay Rd.
2.0 mi
MF
LAKE FOREST

HIGHLAND PARK / HIGHWOOD SIDEWALK & STREET CONNECTIONS
Northbound

(Use sidewalks for safety when possible)
Through parking lot area to Elm Place
Cross tracks on Elm to Green Bay Rd.
North on Green Bay to Prairie Ave.
West on Prairie to Western Ave.
North on Western to North Ave.
West on North to Summit Ave., then Kren Ave.
East on Hyacinth Place to Western Ave.
North to Old Elm Rd. and then east across the tracks. Through the parking lot north and continue on the trail.

Deerpath Ave.
Skokie Hwy.
2.5 mi
Westleigh
Old Elm Rd
Sheridan Rd.
Fort Sheridan
HIGHWOOD
MF
43
1.5 mi
Prairie Ave. 22
Trail crosses over tracks (to west side) at Old Elm Rd.

MATCH   LINE
MILE SCALE
0   1   2   3   4   5

ROUTE SLIP	INTERVAL	TOTAL
Forest Ave. (Wilmette)		
Willow Rd. (Winnetka)	1.7	1.7
Dundee Rd. Rte. 68 (Glencoe)	3.0	4.7
Lake Cook Rd. (Highland Park)	1.2	5.9
Deerfield Rd.	2.5	8.4
Prairie Ave. (Highwood)	1.5	9.9
Old Elm Rd.	1.5	11.4
Deerpath Ave. (Lake Forest)	2.5	13.9
Rockland Road (176)	2.0	15.9

There are approximately 3.5 miles of limestone screenings. The remainder is paved, or street/sidewalk connections.

Screenings:

Glencoe

- Scott Ave. and Harbor St. (.4 mi.)
- South Ave. and Hazel Ave. (.2 mi.)
- Maple Hill Rd. & Ravinia Park (1.1 mi.)

Highland Park

- Ravinia Park to Laurel (2 mi.)

MATCH LINE

The Green Bay Trail runs primarily along the Chicago and Northwestern rail line, from Wilmette to Lake Bluff. Occasionally the biker must ride through parking lots or on streets and sidewalks in communities along the trail.

FACILITIES

🔧	Bike Repair
MF	Multi Facilities Available

Refreshments	First Aid
Telephone	Picnic
Restrooms	Lodging

MILE SCALE

0 1 2 3 4 5

Green Bay Trail

Green Belt Forest Preserve

Trail Length	Approximately 4 miles, 5 miles of looped trails
Surface	Crushed gravel
Uses	Leisure bicycling, cross country skiing, hiking
Location & Setting	The Greenbelt Forest Preserve is nestled between the cities of Waukegan and North Chicago, east of Route 41 and south of Route 120.
Information	Lake County Forest Preserve (847) 367-6640 2000 N. Milwaukee Avenue Libertyville, IL 60048
County	Lake

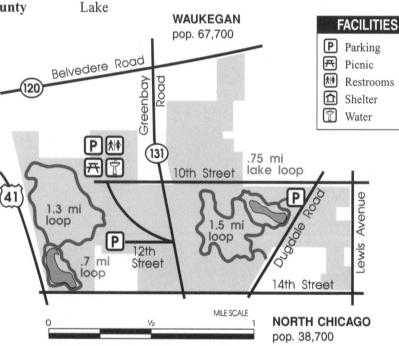

WAUKEGAN
pop. 67,700

Belvedere Road

120

Greenbay Road

131

10th Street

.75 mi lake loop

41

1.3 mi loop

.7 mi loop

P

12th Street

1.5 mi loop

P

Dugdale Road

14th Street

Lewis Avenue

MILE SCALE

0   ½   1

NORTH CHICAGO
pop. 38,700

FACILITIES

P	Parking
🎪	Picnic
🚻	Restrooms
🏠	Shelter
🚰	Water

Entrances- West Section: off Green Bay Road
(Route 131) & 12th Street (open May - Nov)
East Section: Dugdale Road, south of 10th Street
(open year round)

ROUTES

――――	Bicycling Trail
▬▪▬▪▬	Bikeway
▬ ▬ ▬	Alternate Use Trail
▬▬▬▬	Roadway

Greene Valley Forest Preserve

Trail Length	6.2 miles	
Surface	Gravel, mowed turf	
Uses	Fat tire bicycling, cross country skiing, hiking, horseback riding	
Location & Setting	Greene Valley Forest Preserve is located in far south central DuPage County, on Greene Road, ½ mile south of 75th Street. 1,400 acres of woodlands and grasslands.	
Information	Forest Preserve District of DuPage County (630) 790-4900 185 Spring Avenue Glen Ellyn, IL 60138	
County	DuPage	

Trails are symbol coded and may be traveled in both directions. Loop trails range from 1.75 to 6.25 miles.

LISLE
pop. 13,720

75th
75th St.

NAPERVILLE
pop. 90,300

Hinterlong
Forest
Preserve

Wehrli Rd.

Ranchview Dr.

79th St.

E. Branch DuPage River

Auburn Ave.

Thunderbird Rd.

53

Yackley Ave.

Greene Rd.

Wehrli Rd.

Linkage
Trail

Access on:

Thunderbird Road
70th Street
Greene Road between Hobson
Road and 75th Street.

N
W—E
S

Wehrli Rd.

DuPage County
Will County

Royce Rd.

WOODRIDGE
pop. 21,800

53

MILE SCALE

0   ½   1

Heartland Pathways

Trail Length	31 miles
Surface	Ballast
Uses	Fat tire bicycling, hiking
Location & Setting	An abandoned railbed that runs from Clinton to Seymour in east central Illinois. Its 100 foot wide corridor contains one of the last remnants of tall grass prairies in Illinois.
Information	Heartland Pathways (217) 351-1911 119 North Market Street Champaign, IL 61820
County	DeWitt, Pratt, Champaign

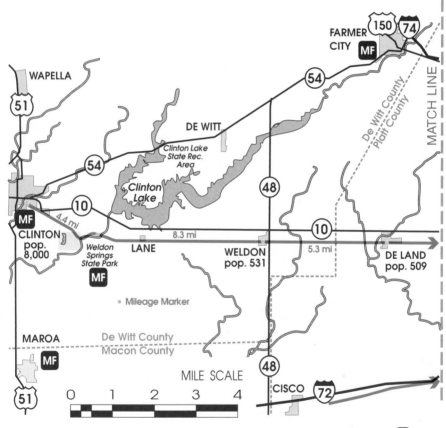

Access can be achieved at connecting roads.
There is no designated parking.

FACILITIES

+ First Aid

MF Multi Facilities Available

Refreshments	First Aid
Telephone	Picnic
Restrooms	Lodging

The Heartland Pathways promotes the observation and conservation of the natural and cultural landscapes of Illinois.

ROUTES

Bicycling Trail
Alternate Use Trail
Roadway

Points of interests include a railroad museum in Monticello and the Allerton Park country estate with its formal gardens, statuary, pools and hiking trails, just west of Monticello.

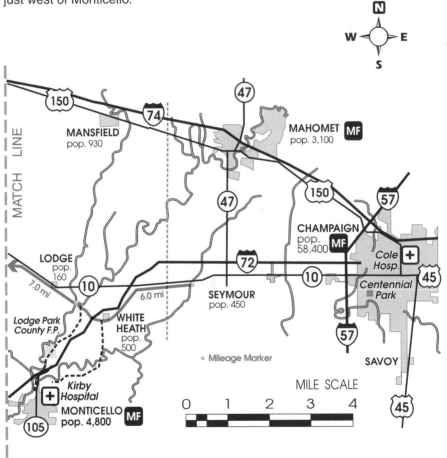

Heartland Pathways

Hennepin Canal Parkway

Trail Length	104.5 miles	
Surface	17 miles of hard surface; 3 miles oil & chip; 14 miles of ad-lime from Lock 33 to Route 92; remainder mowed.	
Uses	Fat tire bicycling, cross country skiing, hiking, horseback riding (except from Bridge 43 to 45).	
Location & Setting	The Hennepin Canal Parkway is a unique linear waterway corridor in northwestern Illinois. The main line of the waterway extends from the great bend of the Illinois River to the Mississippi River, west of Milan.	
Information	Illinois Dept. of Conservation 524 S. Second Street Springfield, IL 62701-1787	
	Site Superintendant RR2 Sheffield, IL 61361	815/454-2328
County	Bureau, Henry, Lee Rock Island, Whiteside.	

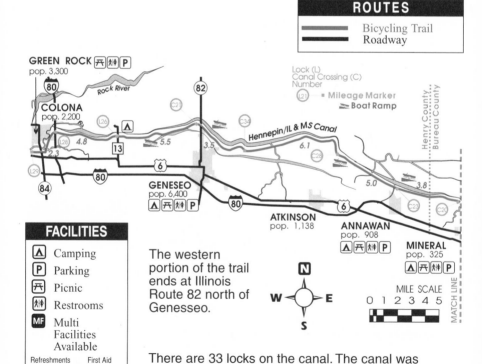

ROUTES

Bicycling Trail
Roadway

GREEN ROCK 🎪🚻P
pop. 3,300

Rock River

COLONA
pop. 2,200

Lock (L)
Canal Crossing (C)
Number
■ Mileage Marker
Boat Ramp

Henry County
Bureau County

Hennepin/IL & MS Canal

GENESEO
pop. 6,400
🏕🎪🚻P

ATKINSON
pop. 1,138

ANNAWAN
pop. 908
🏕🎪🚻P

MINERAL
pop. 325
🏕🎪🚻P

MATCH LINE

FACILITIES

🏕	Camping
P	Parking
🎪	Picnic
🚻	Restrooms
MF	Multi Facilities Available

Refreshments   First Aid
Telephone   Picnic
Restrooms   Lodging

The western portion of the trail ends at Illinois Route 82 north of Genesseo.

N
W—E
S

MILE SCALE
0 1 2 3 4 5

There are 33 locks on the canal. The canal was completed in 1907, but was only used for a short while before being replaced by the railroad.

The parkway is a popular recreatonal area for pleasure boating, picnicking, primitive camping, horseback riding, snowmobiling, backpacking, and hiking in addition to bicycling. A feeder from the Rock River connects to the main line between Sheffield and Mineral. There are numerous parking areas and road accesses along the parkway.

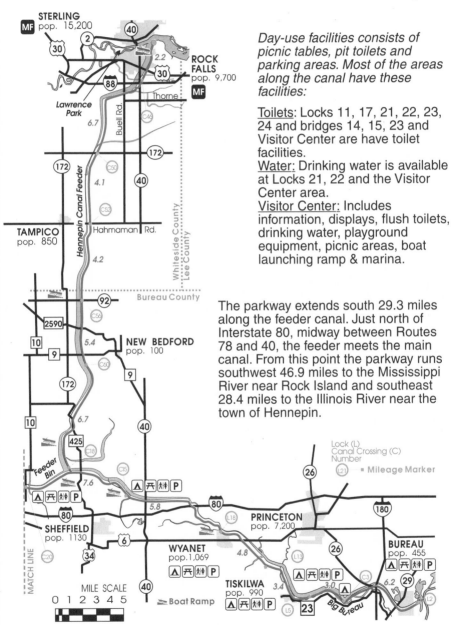

Day-use facilities consists of picnic tables, pit toilets and parking areas. Most of the areas along the canal have these facilities:

Toilets: Locks 11, 17, 21, 22, 23, 24 and bridges 14, 15, 23 and Visitor Center are have toilet facilities.
Water: Drinking water is available at Locks 21, 22 and the Visitor Center area.
Visitor Center: Includes information, displays, flush toilets, drinking water, playground equipment, picnic areas, boat launching ramp & marina.

The parkway extends south 29.3 miles along the feeder canal. Just north of Interstate 80, midway between Routes 78 and 40, the feeder meets the main canal. From this point the parkway runs southwest 46.9 miles to the Mississippi River near Rock Island and southeast 28.4 miles to the Illinois River near the town of Hennepin.

Hennepin Canal Parkway

Herrick Lake Forest Preserve

Trail Length	4.0 miles
Surface	Limestone screenings
Uses	Leisure bicycling, cross country skiing, hiking/ jogging, horseback riding.
Location & Setting	Located in central DuPage County, between Winfield and Naperville. Access from Herrick Road or Butterfield Road. Herrick Lake has 760 acres with a 21 acre lake.
Information	Forest Preserve District of DuPage County (630) 790-4900 185 Spring Avenue Glen Ellyn, IL 60138
County	DuPage

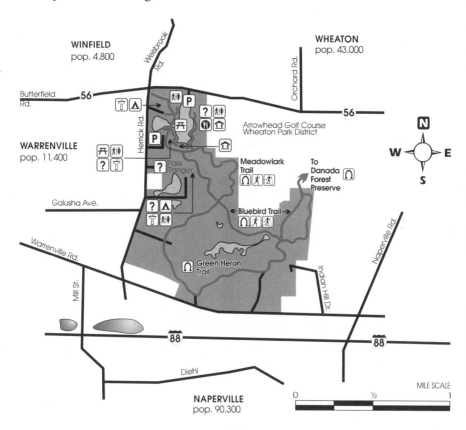

There is a concession building on the eastern shore of the lake.
Canoes and row boats are available for rental.

Hononegah Recreation Path

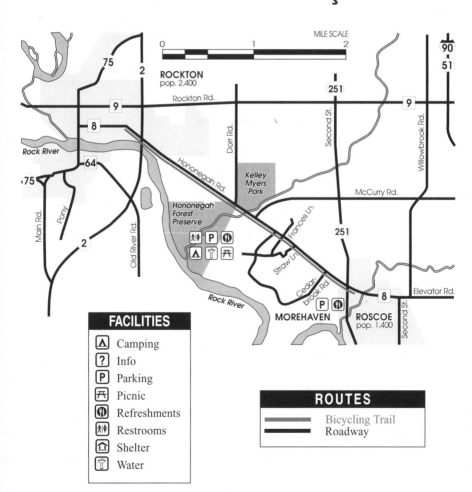

Trail Length   2.5 miles

Surface   Asphalt

Uses   Leisure bicycling, in-line skating, hiking

Location & Setting   The path runs along the south side of Hononegah Road between Hwy. 251 and proceeds northwest ¼ mile west of Route 2. Open area with small communities at either end.

Information   Rockford Park District   (815) 987-8865
1401 North Second Street
Rockford, IL 61107-3086

County   Winnebago

N
W E
S

MILE SCALE
0   1   2

ROCKTON pop. 2,400

Rockton Rd.

Rock River

Hononegah Rd.

Kelley Myers Park

Hononegah Forest Preserve

Dorr Rd.

Second St.

Willowbrook Rd.

McCurry Rd.

Frances Ln.

Straw Ln.

Cedarbrook Rd.

Elevator Rd.

Rock River

Main Rd.

Pony

Old River Rd.

MOREHAVEN

ROSCOE pop. 1,400

Second St.

FACILITIES

- 🏕 Camping
- ? Info
- P Parking
- 🪑 Picnic
- 🍴 Refreshments
- 🚻 Restrooms
- 🏠 Shelter
- 🚰 Water

ROUTES

Bicycling Trail
Roadway

I & M Canal State Trail

Trail Length	56 miles
Surface	Limestone screenings
Uses	Leisure bicycling, cross country skiing, hiking, snowmobiling
Location & Setting	In northeast Illinois, the eastern trailhead begins at the Channanon access. The trail proceeds west to the city of LaSalle, where there are multiple access points and parking. Rural landscape, prairie, small communities
Information	I & M Canal NHC (815) 740-2047 30 North Bluff St. Joliet, IL 60435
County	Will, Grundy, LaSalle

BUFFALO ROCK STATE PARK

Directions: Boyce Memorial Drive south to Ottawa Avenue. West 1.8 miles, past Naplate, to the park entrance. Located five miles from the Fox River Aqueduct on the north bank of the Illinois River. Atop the sandstone bluff at the summit of Buffalo Rock is a sweeping view of the Illinois River. It has several picnic areas.

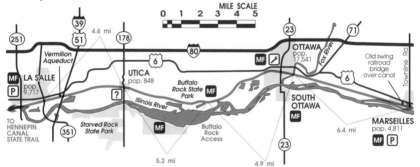

LA SALLE—
Parking off
Canal St.
one half
block south
of Joliet St.

OTTAWA— Sight of
the first Lincoln-
Douglas Debate,
Reddick Mansion,
Fox River Aqueduct
and other historic
attractions.

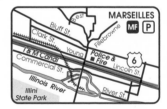

One of the largest earth sculptures ever built, the Effigy Tumuli is located near the park. This reclaimed mine site has turned a barren wasteland into an area filled with recreational opportunities and interesting landscapes. It contains five large earthen figures (effigies) of native aquatic animals. Represented in geometric forms are a water strider, frog, catfish, turtle and a snake.

A series of 17 trails and road segments covering several hundred miles looping Northern Illinois. Some of the proposed route is still conceptual, with linkages to trails via lightly traveled roads and streets.

CENTENNIAL TRAIL—A 3.5 mile multi-use trail, extending from 135th St. in Romeoville north to the Will and Cook County line. The trail runs along the Des Plaines River and the Old Chicago Sanitary and Ship Canal.

CHANNANON STATE PARK—Located near Channahon in Will County, it is the sight of two of the I & M Canal locks and the restored locktender's house. The park provides opportunities for picnicking, tent camping, fishing and canoeing.

Bicyclists can take advantage of the groomed towpath to enjoy the natural and manmade wonders. The trail is marked and has various wayside exhibits that describe features of the canal era.

FACILITIES

🔧	Bike Repair
?	Info
P	Parking
MF	Multi Facilities Available

Refreshments   First Aid
Telephone   Picnic
Restrooms   Lodging

CHANNANON ACCESS—Exit Hwy. 6 at Canal St. Proceed one half mile southeast to Story St., then one block west.

AUX SABLE—This access area is eight miles from Channahon where an aqueduct, lock and locktender's house can be found.

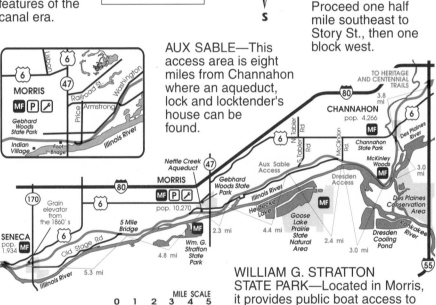

WILLIAM G. STRATTON STATE PARK—Located in Morris, it provides public boat access to the Illinois River. Picnicking and fishing are popular here.

GEBHARD WOODS STATE PARK—Thirty acres of slightly rolling terrain dotted with many stately shade trees.

The I&M (Illinois and Michigan) Canal provided the first complete water route from the east coast to the Gulf of Mexico by connecting Lake Michigan to the Mississippi River by way of the Illinois River.

ROUTES

▬▬▬	Bicycling Trail
▬▬▬	Roadway

I & M Canal State Trail

Illinois Beach State Park

Trail Length	8 miles
Surface	Limestone screenings, packed earth
Uses	Leisure bicycling, cross country skiing, hiking/jogging
Location & Setting	Parallels the Lake Michigan shoreline from south of Zion to the Wisconsin State line. Separating the Northern and Southern Units is Commonwealth Edison's power plant. The Northern unit includes the North Point Marina. Additional trail development is planned.

Northern Unit—The path runs from the Marina to San Pond and to the railroad tracks near 7th St. in Winthrop Harbor.
Southern Unit —The path extends along 29th Street to connect to the Zion Bikeway.

Information	Zion Beach State Park Zion, IL 60099 (847) 662-4811
County	Lake

Wisconsin

Spring Bluff/
Lake County
Forest Preserve

Main

7th St

WINTHROP HARBOR MF 137
pop. 5,500

Entrance

17th St

21st St

Shiloh

Blvd

Power
Plant

MF **ZION**
pop. 19,600 (137)

Wadsworth

LAKE
MICHIGAN

Entrance

Old Beach
Rd

Sheridan

Overlooks

N
W—E
S

ROUTES

———— Biking Trail
▬▬▬ Bikeway
▬ ▬ ▬ Alternate Bike Trail
━ ━ ━ Alternate Use Trail
═══ Planned Trail
━━━━ Roadway

TRAIL USES

 Mountain Biking

 Leisure Biking

 In Line Skating

 (X-C) Cross-Country Skiing

 Hiking

 Horseback Riding

 Snowmobiling

FACILITIES

🔧 Bike Repair

⛺ Camping

➕ First Aid

❓ Info

🛏 Lodging

🅿 Parking

🏕 Picnic

🍺 Refreshments

🚻 Restrooms

🏠 Shelter

🚰 Water

MF Multi Facilities Available

Refreshments	First Aid
Telephone	Picnic
Restrooms	Lodging

ROAD RELATED SYMBOLS

(45) Interstate Highway

(45) U.S. Highway

(45) State Highway

45 County Highway

AREA DESCRIPTIONS

▮ Parks, Schools, Preserves, etc.

▮ Waterway

▬ Mileage Scale

 Directional

DuPage County Great Western Trail opened in 1992. There remains gaps in the Lombard area at St. Charles Road, the Chicago & NorthWestern Railroad, Grace Street, Park Street, and I-355.

ELGIN BRANCH

ROUTE SLIP	SEGMENT	TOTAL
HWY 38 (Wheaton)		
Jewel Rd. (Wheaton)	1.2	1.2
Prince Crossing	3.6	4.8
Smith Road	2.5	7.3
HWY 25 (S. Elgin)	4.3	11.6
HWY 20 (Elgin)	2.8	14.4
Prairie St. (Elgin)	1.8	16.2

The trail crosses numerous residential streets at grade and several four-lane arterials. There are bridges over the DuPage River (both east & west branch), Klein Creek and a small tributary.

Prairie St.
E.Chicago Street
Prairie St.
1.8 mi
25
20
31
20
59
ELGIN
2.8 mi
Stearns Road
Kenyon
Middle St
St Gilbert
25
Powis Rd
Pratts Wayne Woods
MF
4.3 mi
Dunham Road
WAYNE
Smith Rd
Army Trail Road
Elgin Branch
Leroy Oakes Forest Preserve
Great Western Bicycle Trail
Fox River Trail
Smith Rd
Smith Rd
North Ave
Bridge
DuPage County Great Western Trail
4.8 mi
Gary Ave.
Schmale Rd.
64
ST. CHARLES
WEST CHICAGO
2.5 mi
Prince Crossing
Timber Ridge Preserve
County Farm Rd
Pleasant Hill Road
St.Charles Road
Geneva Rd
MATCH LINE
38
Riverside Park
Bennett Park
Kirk Rd
Geneva Spur
West Chicago Prairie
High Lake Rd
Jewel Rd
Main St
GENEVA
Fabyan Forest Preserve
P
West DuPage Woods Preserve
38
WINFIELD
P
WHEATON
MF
Randall Road
Fabyan Pkwy
5.0 mi
BATAVIA
Wilson Rd
Roosevelt Rd
Warrick
Manchester
Wilson Rd
Island Park
31
Pine St
Batavia Rd
Roy C. Blackwell Preserve
Atten Park
P
Orchard Road
Naperville Rd
56
W. Fox River Trail
Hart Road
Roddant Rd
Kirk Rd
Fermilab (see inset)
Batavia Spur
Butterfield
3.5 mi
2.5 mi
Weisbrook Rd
WARRENVILLE
Red Oak Nature Center
56
Church
Bilter Rd
P
59
MF
Warrenville Grove Preserve
Aurora Road
Herrick Lake Preserve
Warrenville Rd
Danada Preserve
Devils Cave
88
Ferry Rd
EAST-WEST TOLLWAY
88
88
25
Aurora Branch
Molitor Rd
P
Diehl Rd
McDowell Grove Preserve
Ogden Ave
Indian Trail Rd.
Batavia Junction (detour-see inset map)
Eola Road
34
NAPERVILLE
N
Indian Creek
Farnsworth Rd
2.5 mi
W E
Illinois Ave.
To The Virgil Gilman Bicycle Trail
25
AURORA
2.3 mi
2.2 mi
S

MILE SCALE
0 1 2 3 4 5

Illinois Prairie Path
Batavia Spur
Great Western Trail-DuPage County

AURORA BRANCH

ROUTE SLIP	SEGMENT	TOTAL
HWY 38 (Wheaton)		
Weisbrook Road	2.5	2.5
Ferry Rd. & HWY 59	3.5	6.0
Eola Rd.	2.5	8.5
Farnsworth Rd. (Aurora)	2.2	10.7
Illinois Ave. (Aurora)	2.3	13.0

Illinois Prairie Path
Batavia Spur
Great Western Trail-DuPage County

Trail Length	Illinois Prairie Path	30.0 miles
	Batavia Spur	5.0 miles
	Great Western Trail	11.4 miles

Surface — Limestone screenings (Batavia Spur is partially paved)

Uses — Leisure bicycling, cross country skiing, hiking/jogging (horseback riding limited)

Location & Setting — Refer to route slips for location of trails. Prairie, wetlands, open spaces, woods, urban communities.

Information — The Illinois Prairie Path
616 Delles Road
Wheaton, IL 60189

(630) 665-5310

N
W—E
S

County — Cook, DuPage, Kane

THE ILLINOIS PRAIRIE PATH MAIN STEM

ROUTE SLIP	SEGMENT	TOTAL
HWY 38 (Wheaton)		
Main St. (Glen Ellyn)	2.7	2.7
Du Page River (E. Branch)	1.6	4.3
Westmore Ave. (Lombard)	2.2	6.5
Salt Creek	2.0	8.5
HWY 290 (Elmhurst)	1.8	10.3
Addison Creek	2.7	13.0
First Ave. (Maywood)	2.0	15.0

MATCH LINE

Along much of The Illinois Prairie Path, nature is abundant. Pheasants, flickers, robins, cardinals, chickadees and goldfinch can be found. Many different species of plants are found throughout the seasons. During spring look for mayapples, which look like small green umbrellas popping out of the ground. In summer, violets and onions are in bloom. Autumn brings out goldenrod and asters.

Indian Boundry Division

Trail Length	10 .8 miles
Surface	Natural groomed
Uses	Fat tire bicycling, hiking, horseback riding
Location & Setting	Located along the east bank of the Des Plaines River in northwest Cook County. The trail begins at Madison Street, east of First Avenue in Maywood, and follows the Des Plaines River north to Touhy Avenue, east of the Tri-State Tollway in Des Plaines.
Information	Emergency Assistance 911
	Cook County Forest Preserve District (708) 366-9420 536 North Harlem Avenue River Forest, IL 60305
County	Cook

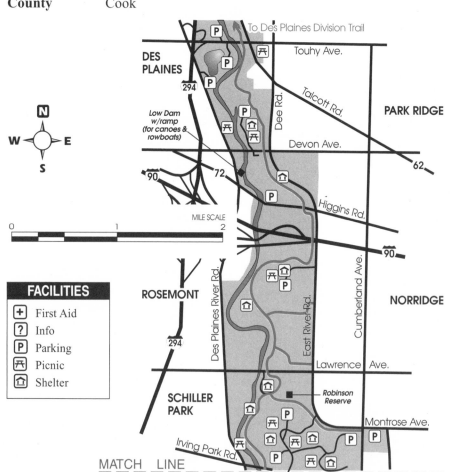

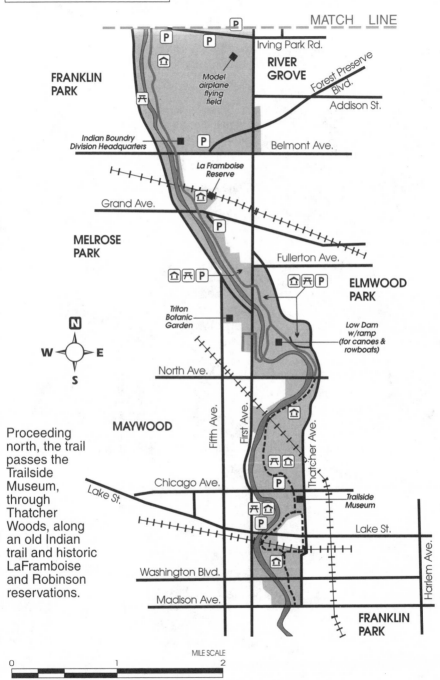

ROUTES

Bicycling Trail
Alternate Use Trail
Roadway

The trail connects to the Salt Creek Forest Preserve to the south and to the Des Plaines River Division to the north.

Irving Park Rd.

FRANKLIN PARK

RIVER GROVE

Forest Preserve Blvd.

Model airplane flying field

Addison St.

Indian Boundry Division Headquarters

Belmont Ave.

La Framboise Reserve

Grand Ave.

MELROSE PARK

Fullerton Ave.

ELMWOOD PARK

N
W E
S

Triton Botanic Garden

Low Dam w/ramp (for canoes & rowboats)

North Ave.

Proceeding north, the trail passes the Trailside Museum, through Thatcher Woods, along an old Indian trail and historic LaFramboise and Robinson reservations.

MAYWOOD

Fifth Ave.

First Ave.

Thatcher Ave.

Chicago Ave.

Lake St.

Trailside Museum

Lake St.

Harlem Ave.

Washington Blvd.

Madison Ave.

FRANKLIN PARK

MILE SCALE

0   1   2

Indian Boundry Division

Kankakee River State Park

Trail Length	8 miles
Surface	Natural groomed
Uses	Fat tire bicycling, cross country skiing, hiking, horseback riding
Location & Setting	Located about 8 miles northwest of Kankakee in northeast Illinois. The park consists of some 4,000 acres with Routes 102 on the north and 113 on the south. Both I-55 and I-57 provide convenient accesses. Straddles the Kankakee River - bluffs, canyons, heavy woods.
Information	Kankakee River State Park (815) 933-1383 P.O. Box 37 Bourbonnais, IL 60914
County	Will

The bicycle trails begins at Davis Creek Area and travels to the Chippewa Campground. At one point it crosses a suspension bridge. The are 12 miles of cross country ski trails, and a 3 miles hiking trail with views of limestone canyons and a frothy waterfall. There is also a 12 mile equestrian trail.

SEE PAGE 77 FOR LEGENDS

Canoe rentals are available at Bird Park in Kankakee (815) 932-6555. It's a four to six hour trip to the park from there. There is a concession stand, camping and picnicking areas. Bicycle rentals are available (815/932-3337).

Kickapoo State Park

Trail Length	6.5 miles (loops)
Surface	Natural - groomed
Uses	Fat tire bicycling (difficult), x-c skiing, hiking
Location & Setting	Located in west central Illinois, 10 miles west of Indiana and 35 miles east of Champaign/Urbana. Kickapoo State Park consists of 2,842 acres and has 22 deep water ponds. The setting is made up of lushly forested uplands and bottomlands along the Middle Fork of the Vermilion River. There is easy access from I-74 and connecting roads surrounding the park.
Information	Kickapoo State Park (717) 442-4915 10906 Park Road Oakwood, IL 61858
County	Vermilion

Kickapoo owes its crystal clear pond and forested ridges to the regenerative powers of nature, which reclaimed the area over the past 50 years after a century of strip mining.

Activities include hiking, canoeing, camping, horseback riding, scuba diving, in addition to bicycling.

2050 N.

Road 900 E.

P

Out & Back Trail 6.5 mi.

6.5 mi.

P

Stump Pond

Road 1180 E.

Road 2000 N.

To Rte. 136 & Henning 10.5 miles

1200

Johnson Hill Bridge

970

Little Hook Lake Possum Pond

Emerald Pond

Road 1950 N.

Inland Sea

Clear Lake

Riverview Trail 3.0 mi.

Road 1000 N.

1

Road 850 E.

Road 1880 N.

Road 1000 E.

1450

P

Park Office

?

N
W — E
S

1950

To Danville (pop. 39,000) 2 miles

Nature Trail .75 mi.

High Pond Trail .75 mi.

To Champaign (pop. 58,400) Urbana (pop. 36,000) 35 mi.

EXIT 206
To Oakwood

74

Vermilion River Middle Fork

Long Lake

Deep Pond

74

EXIT 210

To Indiana 10 miles

MILE SCALE
0   ½   1

1180   150

Kiwanis Trail

Trail Length	6.5 miles
Surface	Paved (10 feet), connecting low speed streets
Uses	Leisure bicycling, cross country skiing, in-line skating, hiking
Location & Setting	Located on the north side of the Rock River in Moline. It extends from 7th Street to 60th.
Information	Moline Park and Recreation Department (309) 797-0785 3300 Fifth Avenue Moline, IL 61265
County	Rock Island

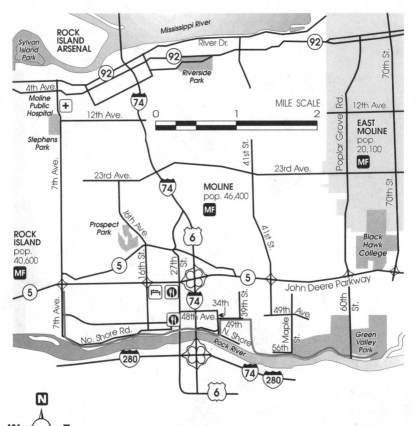

The trail is open from sunrise to sunset, year round.
Food, lodging, sight-seeing facilities are readily available.

Long Prairie Trail

Trail Length	7.5 miles
Surface	Asphalt
Uses	Leisure bicycling, in-line skating, cross country skiing, hiking
Location & Setting	The east trailhead is on County Line Road about a half mile north of Hwy. 173. The entrance is on the left and there is ample parking. The west trailhead is on Hwy. 76 about a mile west of Poplar Grove. Open areas, farmland, small communities.
Information	Boone County Conservation District (815) 547-7935 7600 Appleton Road Belvidere. IL 61008
County	Boone

Although there are no designated facilities along the trail, there are services available in the communities of Poplar Grove and Capron. The nearby cities of Belvidere and Rockford offer ample lodging and restaurants.

You will find many markers along the trail describing the local area and other points of interest.

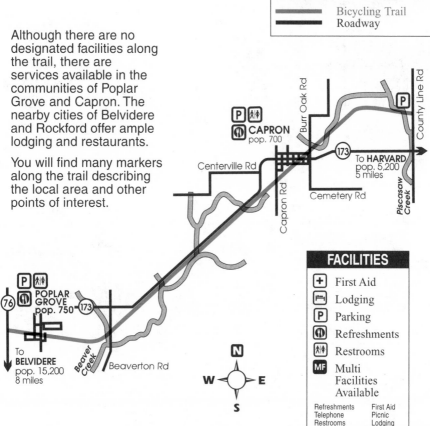

Lowell Parkway

Trail Length	3 miles
Surface	Screenings
Uses	Leisure bicycling, hiking/jogging, cross-country skiing, horseback riding & snowmobiling
Location & Setting	Located in the town of Dixon in northwest Illinois. The path is a converted railbed.
Information	Dixon Park District (815) 284-3306 804 Palmyra Avenue Dixon, IL 61021
County	Lee

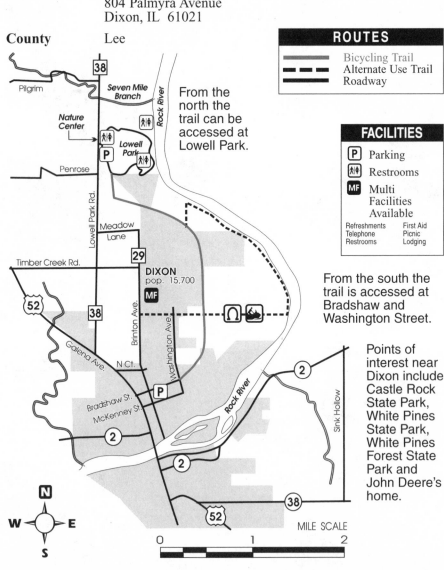

ROUTES

Bicycling Trail
Alternate Use Trail
Roadway

FACILITIES

P Parking

Restrooms

MF Multi Facilities Available

Refreshments   First Aid
Telephone   Picnic
Restrooms   Lodging

From the north the trail can be accessed at Lowell Park.

From the south the trail is accessed at Bradshaw and Washington Street.

Points of interest near Dixon include Castle Rock State Park, White Pines State Park, White Pines Forest State Park and John Deere's home.

MILE SCALE

0   1   2

Miscellaneous Trails

Trail Name   El Paso Trail

Trail Length   2.7 miles

Surface   Crushed stone

Uses   Leisure bicycling, hiking

Location   El Paso

Information   Town of El Paso—City Hall
                    (309) 527-4005
                    52 North Elm
                    El Paso, IL 61738-4005

County   Madison

Trail Name   Pioneer Parkway

Trail Length   2.5 miles

Surface   Crushed stone

Uses   Leisure bicycling, cross country skiing, hiking

Location   From Peoria to Alta

Information   Peoria Park District
                    (309) 682-1200
                    2218 N. Prospect Road
                    Peoria, IL 61603

County   Peoria

Trail Name   Ronald J. Foster Heritage Parkway

Trail Length   3.2 miles

Surface   Asphalt

Uses   Leisure bicycling, cross country skiing, hiking

Location   Glen Carbon

Information   Glen Carbon Village Hall
                    (618) 288-1200
                    151 North Main Street
                    Glen Carbon, IL 62034

County   Madison

McDowell Grove
Forest Preserve

Trail Length	5.6 miles
Surface	Mowed turf
Uses	Fat tire bicycling, cross country skiing, hiking, horseback riding
Location & Setting	This preserve is located in southwest DuPage County on Raymond Road at McDowell Avenue between Ogden Avenue and the East-West Tollway (Hwy. 88) and south of Warrenville.
Information	Forest Preserve District of DuPage County(630) 790-4900 185 Spring Avenue Glen Ellyn, IL 60138
County	DuPage

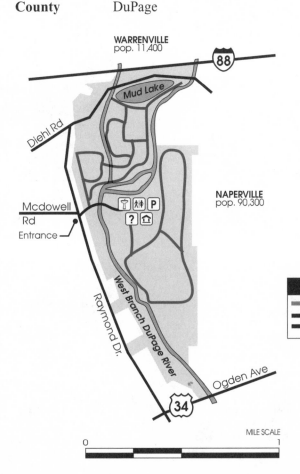

WARRENVILLE
pop. 11,400

88

Mud Lake

Diehl Rd

Mcdowell
Rd
Entrance

NAPERVILLE
pop. 90,300

West Branch DuPage River

Raymond Dr.

Ogden Ave

34

MILE SCALE

0   1

FACILITIES

?	Info
P	Parking
⑩	Refreshments
⚥	Restrooms
⌂	Shelter
▽	Water
MF	Multi Facilities Available

Refreshments   First Aid
Telephone   Picnic
Restrooms   Lodging

ROUTES

▬▬▬	Bicycling Trail
▬ ▬ ▬	Alternate Use Trail
▬▬▬	Roadway

N
W — E
S

Moraine Hills State Park

Trail Length	8.9 miles
Surface	Limestone screenings
Uses	Leisure and fat tire bicycling, hiking
Location & Setting	Located 3 miles south of the city of McHenry, there is an easily recognized sign at the junction of Hwy. 176 and River Road directing you to parking. Wooded, wetlands, and is well groomed with many small hills and curves.
Information	Moraine Hills State Park 914 South River Road McHenry, IL 60050
County	McHenry

(815)385-1624

N W—E S

<u>Trails are one-way and color coded.</u> *There are three loops:*
Lake Defiance- 3.72 miles with red markers
Leather Leaf Bog- 3.18 miles with blue markers
Fox River- 2.0 miles with yellow markers

Moraine Hills State Park consists of 1,690 acres. There is trail access at McHenry Dam.

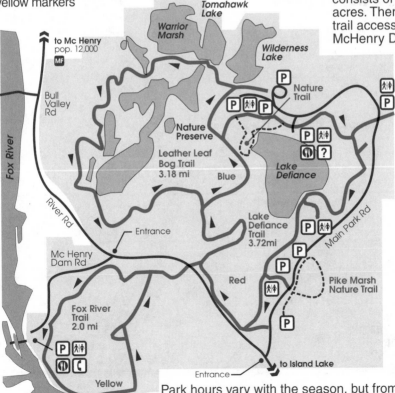

Park hours vary with the season, but from May 1 to August 31, the park is open from 6am to 9pm.

North Branch Bicycle Trail
Techny Trail

Trail Length	20 miles (plus bikeways)
Surface	Paved
Uses	Leisure bicycling, cross country skiing, hiking/jogging
Location & Setting	Open spaces, wooded—extends from the Chicago Botanic Gardens south approximately 20 miles to Caldwell and Devon Avenues in Chicago.
Information	Forest Preserve District of Cook County (708) 366-9420 536 N. Harlem Avenue River Forest, IL 60305
County	Cook

POINTS OF INTEREST

- A Chicago Botanic Garden
- B Skokie Lagoons
- C Blue Star Memorial Woods
- D Glenview Woods
- E Harms Woods
- F Chick Evans Golf Course
- G Linne Woods
- H Miami Woods
- I Clayton Smith Woods
- J Whealan Pool
- K Edgebrook Golf Course
- L Billy Caldwell Golf Course

FACILITIES

[?] Info

MF Multi Facilities Available

Refreshments   First Aid
Telephone   Picnic
Restrooms   Lodging

ROUTES

Bicycling Trail
Bikeway
Alternate Bike Trail
Planned Trail
Roadway

MILE SCALE

0   1   2   3

EMERGENCY ASSISTANCE

Forest Preserve Police at 708/366-8210 or 708/366-8211

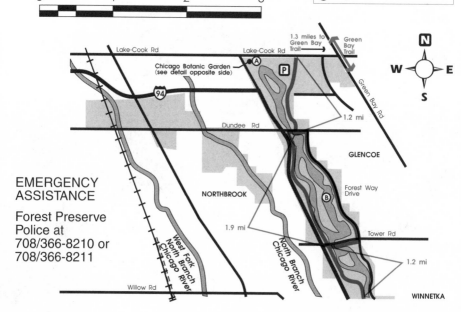

The trail winds along the North Branch of the Chicago River and the Skokie Lagoons, providing access to various picnic groves and communities in addition to the Botanic Gardens.

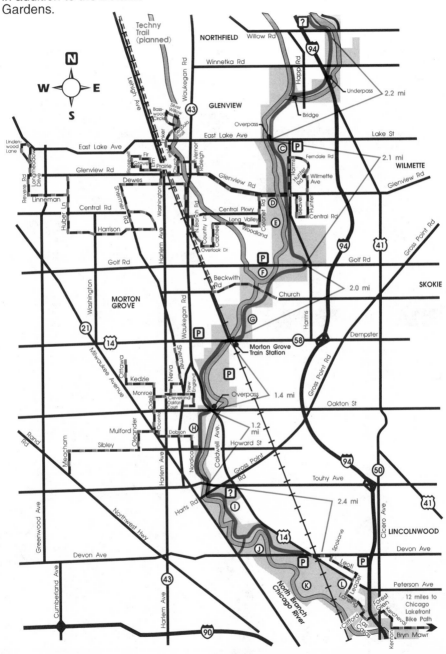

North Branch Bicycle Trail

North Shore Path
Libertyville Trail

Trail Length	15.3 miles north to south, 7.0 miles east to west
Surface	Limestone screenings, paved
Uses	Leisure bicycling, cross country skiing, hiking/jogging
Location & Setting	North/south section—Lake Bluff to Wisconsin state line. East/west section—proceeds west from just south of Rockland Rd. (Hwy. 176) in Lake Bluff to Carmel High School in Mundelein. Surburban, open and lightly wooded areas.
Information	

Lake County Dept. of Transportation   (847) 362-3950
600 W. Winchester Road
Libertyville, IL 60048

County	Lake

MILE SCALE

0   1   2   3   4

MATCH LINE

ROUTES

Bicycling Trail
Alternate Bike Trail
Planned Trail
Roadway

N
W — E
S

41
120
Belvidere Rd
131
14th St
2.5 mi
NO. SHORE PATH

NORTH CHICAGO
pop. 38,800   MF

94
22nd St
M.L. King Dr.

137

137

DES PLAINES RIVER TRAIL

21

Skokie Hwy.

Green Bay Rd

Sheridan Rd.

2.8 mi

LIBERTYVILLE
pop. 16,500   MF

94

LAKE BLUFF
pop. 4,500   MF

176

LIBERTYVILLE TRAIL

176

Rockland Rd

Underpass

131

MF

41

GREEN BAY TRAIL

LAKE FOREST
pop. 15,200

Brice Ave.

Carmel High School

MUNDELEIN
pop. 17,000   MF

Des Plaines River

NORTH SHORE PATH EAST/WEST

DES PLAINES RIVER TRAIL

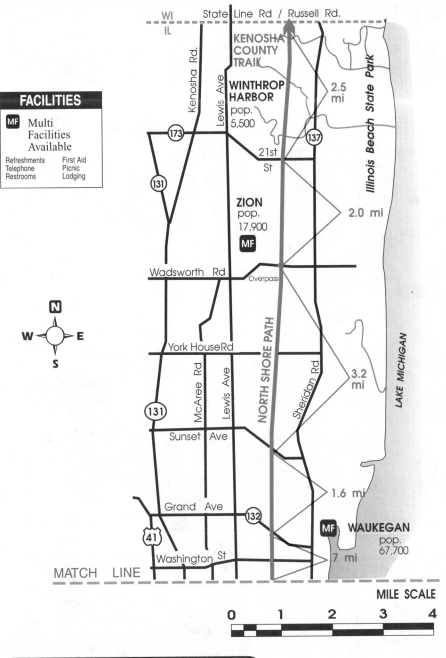

FACILITIES

MF Multi
Facilities
Available

Refreshments	First Aid
Telephone	Picnic
Restrooms	Lodging

State Line Rd / Russell Rd.

WI
IL

KENOSHA
COUNTY
TRAIL

WINTHROP
HARBOR
pop.
5,500

Kenosha Rd.

Lewis Ave

173

131

21st
St

137

2.5
mi

Illinois Beach State Park

ZION
pop.
17,900

MF

2.0 mi

Wadsworth Rd

Overpass

York House Rd

NORTH SHORE PATH

131

McAree Rd

Lewis Ave

Sheridan Rd

3.2
mi

LAKE MICHIGAN

Sunset Ave

Grand Ave

41

132

1.6 mi

MF WAUKEGAN
pop.
67,700

Washington St

7 mi

MATCH LINE

N
W E
S

MILE SCALE

0   1   2   3   4

ROUTE SLIP	INTERVAL	TOTAL
Rockland Rd. (176)		
M.L. King Dr. (No. Chicago)	2.8	2.8
Grand Ave. (Waukegan)	3.2	6.0
Golf Rd./Sunset	1.6	7.6
Wadsworth	3.2	10.8
21st (Hwy. 173)	2.0	12.8
Russell Rd. (state line)	2.5	15.3

North Shore Path
Libertyville Trail

Oak Brook Bike Paths

Trail Length	17 miles (approximately) and some 5+ miles of designated bikeways
Surface	Paved, screenings
Uses	Leisure bicycling, in-line skating, hiking/jogging
Location & Setting	Oak Brook is located in east central DuPage County. The bike paths and bikeways are located throughout Oak Brook. There are multiple accesses to the paths as is parking. The setting is urban, open and wooded.
Information	Oak Brook Park District 1300 Forest Gate Road Oak Brook, IL 60521 (630) 990-4233
County	DuPage

The paths are well marked with signs, and several of the major roads provide tunnels for safe passage across.

Palatine Trail & Bikeway

Trail Length	15 miles (includes connecting bike routes)
Surface	Paved
Uses	Leisure bicycling, cross country skiing, hiking
Location & Setting	Palatine is located in northwest Cook County. Wooded areas, open spaces, connecting street bikeways, urban.
Information	Palatine Park District (847) 991-0333 250 East Wood Street Palatine, IL 60067
County	Cook

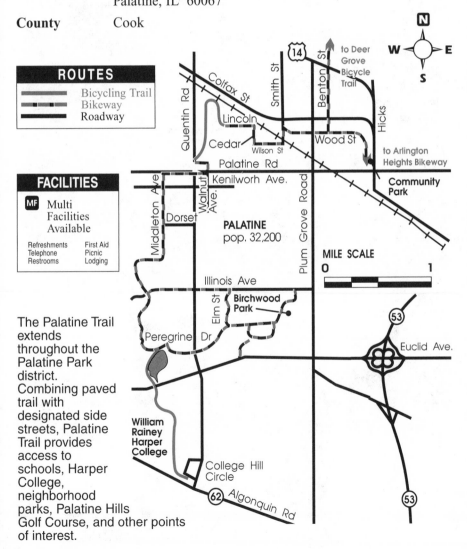

ROUTES
- Bicycling Trail
- Bikeway
- Roadway

FACILITIES

MF Multi Facilities Available

Refreshments First Aid
Telephone Picnic
Restrooms Lodging

The Palatine Trail extends throughout the Palatine Park district. Combining paved trail with designated side streets, Palatine Trail provides access to schools, Harper College, neighborhood parks, Palatine Hills Golf Course, and other points of interest.

Palos & Sag Valley Forest Preserve
I & M Canal Trail—Cook County

Trail Length	Palos = 30.0 miles & I & M Canal = 8.9 miles
Surface	Palos = Natural groomed & I & M Canal = paved
Uses	Palos = Fat tire bicycling, hiking, horseback riding I & M Canal = Leisure bicycling, cross country skiing
Location & Setting	Palos located in southwest Cook County, mostly hilly and forested with many upland meadows, lakes ponds and sloughs. I & M Canal open and flat.
Information	Palos Division Headquarters (708) 839-5617 Willow Springs Road between 95th and 107th St.
County	Cook

ROUTES

Bicycling Trail
Alternate Use Trail
Roadway

MATCH LINE

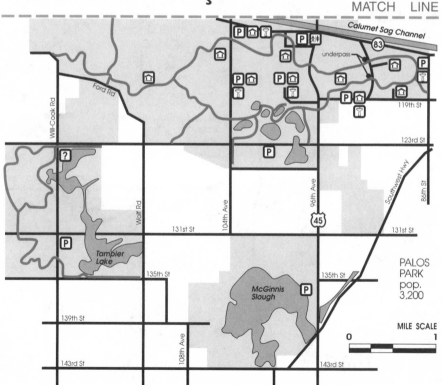

A suggested trail access is by 104th St. (Willow Springs Avenue) and Hwy. 171 (Archer Ave.)

There is a parking lot with the paved trail running through it. Nearby is a visitors center that explains the history of the National Heritage Corridor.

The woodlands provide colorful autumn foliage as well as an abundance of wildlife.

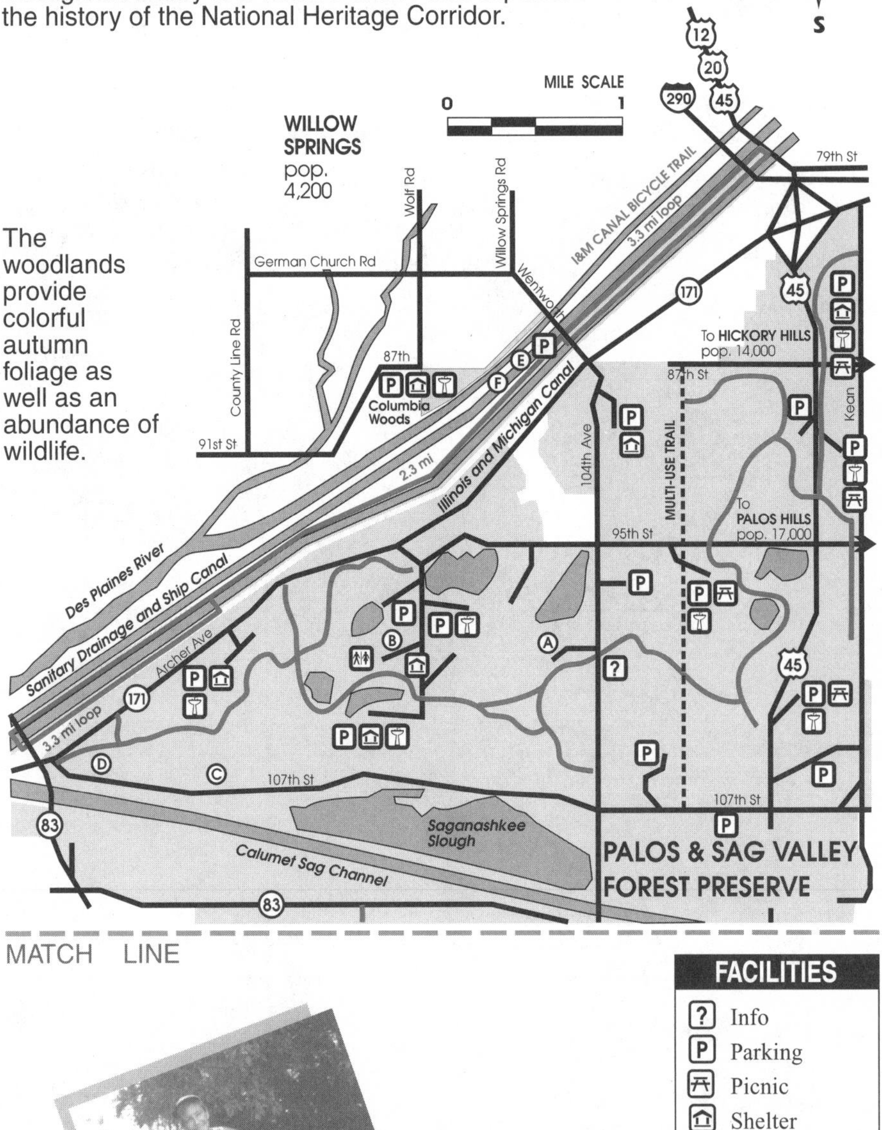

N **W E** **S**

MILE SCALE
0   1

WILLOW SPRINGS
pop. 4,200

Wolf Rd
Willow Springs Rd
German Church Rd
County Line Rd
Wentworth
87th
Columbia Woods
91st St
95th St

I&M CANAL BICYCLE TRAIL
3.3 mi loop

Illinois and Michigan Canal
2.3 mi

Des Plaines River
Sanitary Drainage and Ship Canal

Archer Ave
3.3 mi loop

104th Ave
MULTI-USE TRAIL

To HICKORY HILLS
pop. 14,000
87th St

To PALOS HILLS
pop. 17,000

95th St
107th St

Saganashkee Slough

Calumet Sag Channel

PALOS & SAG VALLEY FOREST PRESERVE

12
20
290
45
79th St
171
45
Kean

83
171
83

A
B
C
D
E
F
?

MATCH   LINE

Palos & Sag Valley Forest Preserve

Peace Road Trail

Trail Length	5 miles
Surface	Screenings
Uses	Leisure bicycling, cross country skiing, hiking
Location & Setting	The Peace Road Trail extends from Bethany Road in Sycamore to Pleasant Street in DeKalb. Current access to the Great Western Trail is by way of Airport Road. The setting is rural with farmland, woods and open areas.
Information	DeKalb County Forest Preserve Commission 110 East Sycamore Street Sycamore, IL 60178 (815) 895-7191
County	DeKalb

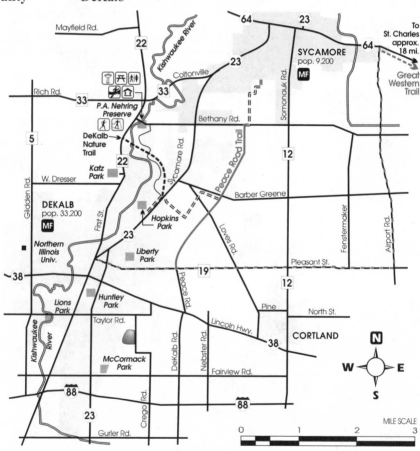

Planned construction includes a path between the Peace Road Trail and both Hopkins Park and the DeKalb Nature Trail. Also planned is an alternate route connecting to the Great Western Trail.

Pecatonica Prairie Path

Trail Length	21 miles
Surface	Ballast
Uses	Fat tire bicycling, hiking
Location & Setting	The trail follows an old railroad right-of-way through Stephenson and Winnebago counties. The eastern trailhead is off Meridian Road just south of Hwy. 20 and west of the city of Rockford. The western trailhead is south of the intersection of Hillcrest Road and River Road, off Hwy. 75, 3 miles east of Freeport. The trails pass through open areas and farmland. Lightly wooded.
Information	Rockford Park District (815) 987-8865 1401 North Second Street Rockford, IL 61107-3086
County	Winnebago, Stephenson

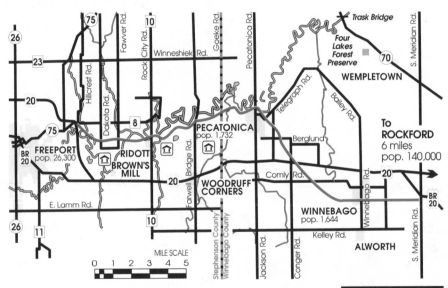

A variety of animals, birds and native wild flowers can be found along the corridor. The right-of-way is owned by Commonwealth Edison, which leases it to Pecatonica Prairie Path, Inc.

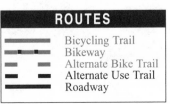

ROUTES

- Bicycling Trail
- Bikeway
- Alternate Bike Trail
- Alternate Use Trail
- Roadway

FACILITIES

- Picnic
- Restrooms
- Shelter
- Water
- **MF** Multi Facilities Available

Refreshments   First Aid
Telephone   Picnic
Restrooms   Lodging

Pere Marquette State Park

Trail Length	11.25 miles
Surface	Natural - groomed
Uses	Fat tire bicycling, hiking, horseback riding.
Location & Setting	East central Illinois overlooking the Mississippi and Illinois Rivers some 20 miles north of St. Louis, Missouri. Entrance to the park is off Route 100 about 6 miles west of Grafton. Setting consists of bluffs, ravines and deep woods.
Information	Pere Marquette State Park (618) 786-3323 Route 100, P.O. Box 158 Grafton, IL 62037
County	Jersey

There is a fully equipped concession stand located at the marina. Overlooking the Mississippi River, this 7,895 acre preservation area was named after Father Jacques Marquette, who along with Louis Joliet were the first group of Europeans to reach the confluence of the Mississippi and Illinois Rivers in 1673. Year round activities include horseback riding, camping, fishing, boating and hiking in addition to mountain bicycling.

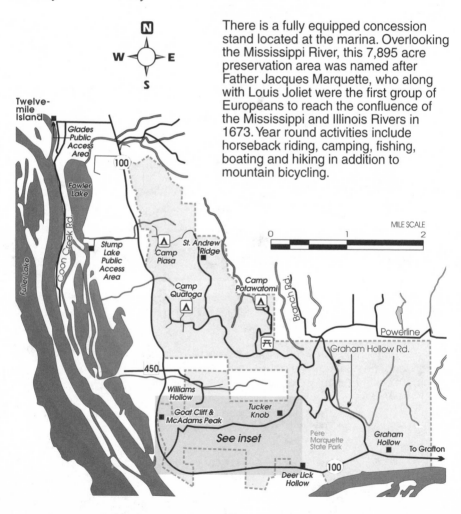

Pere Marquette State Park is noted for its exceptional fall colors, spectacular views ot the Illinois and Missisippi rivers and its bald eagles in winter.

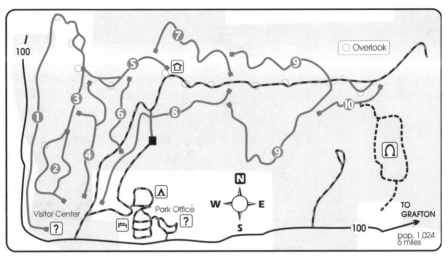

NQ	NAME	COLOR	LENGTH	DIFFICULTY
1	Goat Cliff	Yellow	2 miles	Moderate
2	Dogwood	Dk. Blue	3/4 mile	Moderate
3	Ridge	Lt. Blue	1/2 mile	Difficult
4	Ravine	Green	1 mile	Moderate
5	Hickory (MAIN)	Red	3/4 mile	Easy
6	Oak	Pink	3/4 mile	Moderate
7	Hickory (NORTH)	Red/White Bar	1 mile	Moderate
8	Hickory (SOUTH)	Red/White Circle	1 1/2 miles	Moderate
9	Fern Hollow	Orange	2 1/4 miles	Moderate
10	Rattlesnake	Orange/White Bar	3/4 mile	Moderate

ROUTES

Biking Trail
Bikeway
Roadway

FACILITIES

⌂	Camping
?	Info
⊟	Lodging
开	Picnic
⌂	Shelter
MF	Multi Facilities Available

Refreshments First Aid
Telephone Picnic
Restrooms Lodging

Pere Marquette State Park

Pimiteoui Trail

Trail Length	Approximately 5 miles
Surface	Paved
Uses	Leisure bicycling, hiking/jogging
Location & Setting	Located in the city of Peoria, south to north, from the Robert Mitchell Bridge to the Pioneer Parkway. Urban and open areas.
Information	Peoria Convention & Visitors Bureau (800)747-0302 403 North East. Jefferson Street Peoria, IL 61603
County	Peoria

ROUTES

- Bicycling Trail
- Bikeway
- Alternate Bike Trail
- Roadway

ROUTE SLIP

Foot of Robert Michel Bridge along waterfront to Woodruff Park.

Cross Adams St., and then head east 75 feet to Abington St.

Follow Abington to Perry Ave., in front of Woodruff High School.

Turn north on Perry, through Springdale Cemetery and under Route 150 to Harvard Ave.

Continue on Harvard Ave., north to Lake Ave., then turn right on Prospect Rd.

Follow Prospect Rd. north for 9 blocks to Kingman Ave., and then turn left on Kingman Ave., following it west to Montclair Ave.

Turn right on Montclair and follow it north to Humbolt Ave., and then to Prospect by Junction City.

Continue along the eastern edge of the railway to Pioneer Parkway.

MILE SCALE
0   1   2   3

Prairie Trail—North Extension

🚲 🚵 ⛷ 🚶 ⛩ 🏂

Trail Length	7.5 miles
Surface	Limestone screenings (some ballast)
Uses	Leisure bicycling, fat tire bicycling, cross country skiing, hiking, horseback riding, snowmobiling
Location & Setting	From Ringwood, north of McHenry, to the Wisconsin State Line. Open space, wooded areas, small communities.
Information	McHenry County Conservation District (815) 678-4431 6512 Harts Road Ringwood, IL 60072
County	McHenry

Richmond is an interesting small community with several antique shops. The trail crosses Hwy. 173 just west of Hwy. 31. There is no designated parking.

FACILITIES

P	Parking
🍴	Refreshments
🚻	Restrooms
MF	Multi Facilities Available

Refreshments First Aid
Telephone Picnic
Restrooms Lodging

Fat tires are recommended on the North Extension as the trail is somewhat rough from equestrian use.

Prairie Trail—South Extension

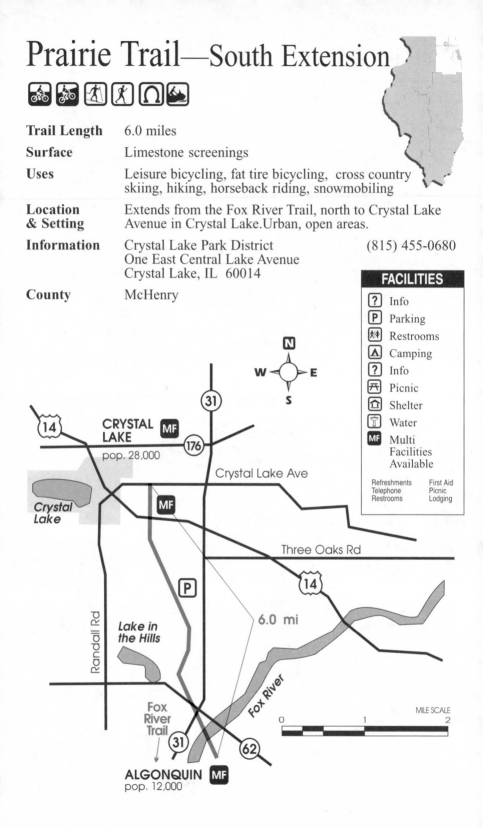

Trail Length	6.0 miles
Surface	Limestone screenings
Uses	Leisure bicycling, fat tire bicycling, cross country skiing, hiking, horseback riding, snowmobiling
Location & Setting	Extends from the Fox River Trail, north to Crystal Lake Avenue in Crystal Lake. Urban, open areas.
Information	Crystal Lake Park District (815) 455-0680 One East Central Lake Avenue Crystal Lake, IL 60014
County	McHenry

FACILITIES

- [?] Info
- [P] Parking
- [⚥] Restrooms
- [△] Camping
- [?] Info
- [⛩] Picnic
- [⌂] Shelter
- [▽] Water
- [MF] Multi Facilities Available

Refreshments   First Aid
Telephone   Picnic
Restrooms   Lodging

N W E S

14 — CRYSTAL LAKE [MF] — pop. 28,000 — 31 — 176

Crystal Lake

Crystal Lake Ave

[MF]

Three Oaks Rd

[P]

14

6.0 mi

Randall Rd

Lake in the Hills

Fox River

Fox River Trail

31 — 62

ALGONQUIN [MF]
pop. 12,000

MILE SCALE
0   1   2

Pratts Wayne Woods Forest Preserve

Trail Length	7.3 miles
Surface	Mowed turf
Uses	Fat tire bicycling, cross country skiing, hiking, horseback riding
Location & Setting	Located in the northwest corner of DuPage County between Wayne and Barlett. Access from Powis Road a mile north of Army Trail Road or from the Illinois Prairie Path. It's 2,600 acres include savannas, marshes, meadows and prairies. Wildlife and plants abound.
Information	Forest Preserve District of DuPage County (630) 790-4900 185 Spring Avenue Glen Ellyn, IL 60138
County	DuPage

A model airplane field is located on the east side of Powis Road in the special use area.

ROUTES

— Bicycling Trail
- - - Alternate Bike Trail
— Roadway

MILE SCALE

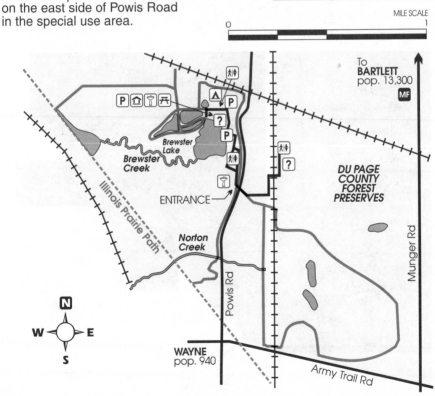

Red Hills State Park

Trail Length	6 miles
Surface	Screenings, natural
Uses	Leisure and fat tire bicycling (moderate) and hiking
Location & Setting	Located in southeastern Illinois between Olney and Lawrenceville on U.S. Route 50. The park consists of 948 acres with wooded hills, deep ravines, meadows and year round springs.
Information	Red Hills State Park Rural Route 2—Box 252A Sumner, IL 62466
	(618) 936-2469
County	Lawrence

Facilities include shaded picnic area with tables and grills, 120 Class A campsites with vehicular access and primitive tent camping. In addition to the bicycling/hiking trail, there is a 5 mile equestrian trail.

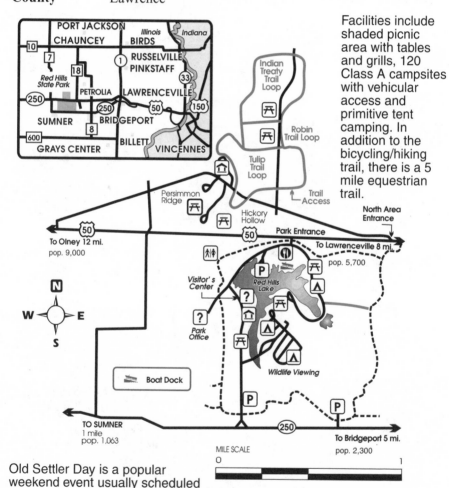

Old Settler Day is a popular weekend event usually scheduled late in April. Red Hill is the highest point of land between St. Louis and Cincinnati. It has a 120 foot tower and cross rising from its summit.

River Trail of Illinois

Trail Length	10.8 miles
Surface	Paved, limestone screenings
Uses	Leisure bicycling, hiking
Location & Setting	Located between Morton and East Peoria. Urban, open and wooded areas, small hills.
Information	Fond Du Lac Park District 201 Veterans Drive East Peoria, IL 61611
County	Tazewell

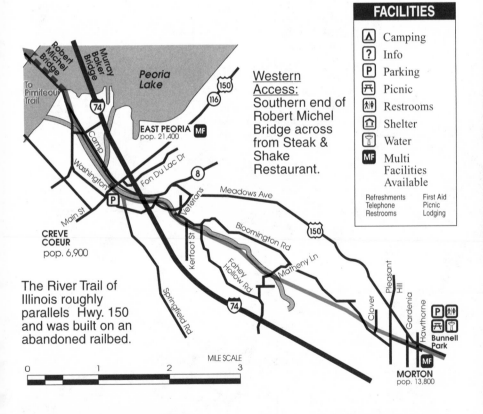

FACILITIES

⚠	Camping
?	Info
P	Parking
🅿	Picnic
👫	Restrooms
🏠	Shelter
🚰	Water
MF	Multi Facilities Available

Refreshments   First Aid
Telephone   Picnic
Restrooms   Lodging

Western Access: Southern end of Robert Michel Bridge across from Steak & Shake Restaurant.

The River Trail of Illinois roughly parallels Hwy. 150 and was built on an abandoned railbed.

MILE SCALE

0   1   2   3

ROUTES

Bicycling Trail
Alternate Bike Trail
Alternate Use Trail
Roadway

N
W — E
S

Eastern Access: Across from K-Mart and Golden Corral Restaurant.

Rock Cut State Park

Trail Length	10 miles
Surface	Dirt
Uses	Fat tire bicycling (easy to moderate), cross country skiing, hiking, horseback riding, snowmobiling
Location & Setting	Located in Winnebago County northeast of Rockford, and approximately 80 miles northwest of Chicago. From I-90, exit at East Riverside Blvd. and head west for 1 mile, then turn right on McFarland Road to Harlem Road (dead end). Turn east (right) for a little over a mile, over I-90, to the Park entrance. Terrain is rugged, rocky with woods and small hills.
Information	Rock Cut State Park 7318 Harlem Road Loves Park, IL 61111 — (815) 885-3311 Emergency 911
County	Winnebago

SEE LEGENDS ON PAGE 77

There are individual routes for hiking, bicycling, horseback riding and snowmobiling. The track varies from 5 to 10 feet wide.

Rock Cut State Park consists of 3,096 acres. Facilities include concessions, restrooms, water, boat rental and canoe access.

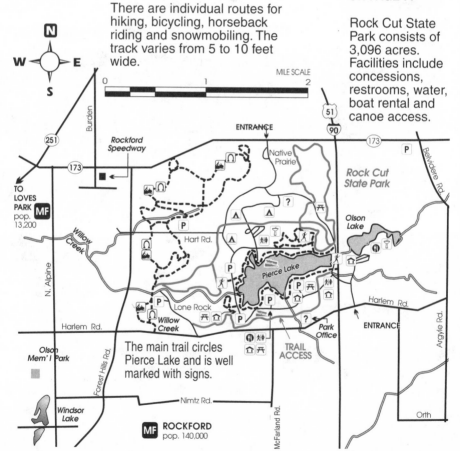

The main trail circles Pierce Lake and is well marked with signs.

Rock River & Sportscore Recreation Path

Trail Length	8 miles
Surface	Asphalt
Uses	Leisure bicycling, in-line skating, cross country skiing, hiking/jogging
Location & Setting	The path follows the Rock River in Rockford from Walnut Street north through Veterans Memorial Park/Sportscore to Harlem Road. The setting is urban.
Information	Rockford Park District 1401 North Second Street Rockford, IL 61107-3086 (815) 987-8865
County	Winnebago

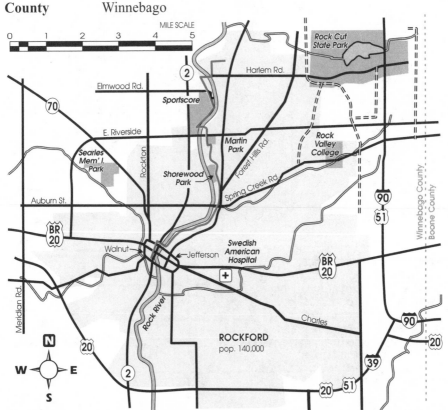

The Sportscore joins the Rock River Path at Elmwood Road, proceeds along Brown Beach Road jogging west, then northeast along Harlem Road and across the Rock River. The path crosses the Rock River at Jefferson Street, Riverside Blvd. and Harlem Road. There are numerous points of interest along the path.

Rock Island State Trail

Trail Length	28.3 miles
Surface	Limestone screenings
Uses	Leisure bicycling, cross country skiing, hiking
Location & Setting	Stretches from Pioneer Parkway along an old railroad right-of-way through the communities of Dunlap, Princeville, and Wyoming to the edge of Toulon in Stark County northwest of Peoria.The Trail lies in a vast plain formerly occupied by tallgrass prairie. The land is dominated by cultivated fields but numerous patches of prairie and stands of trees are scattered along the route.

Information	Friends of the Rock Island Trail	(309) 694-3196
	P.O. Box 272—Peoria, IL 61650	
	Rock Island Trail State Park	(309) 695-2228
	P.O. Box 64—Wyoming, IL 61491	

County	Peoria, Stark

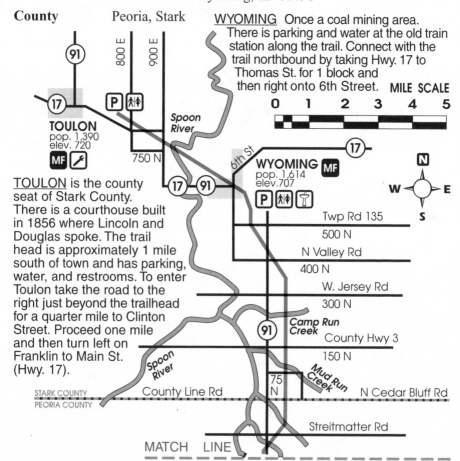

WYOMING Once a coal mining area. There is parking and water at the old train station along the trail. Connect with the trail northbound by taking Hwy. 17 to Thomas St. for 1 block and then right onto 6th Street.

MILE SCALE
0   1   2   3   4   5

TOULON
pop. 1,390
elev. 720

750 N

WYOMING
pop. 1,614
elev. 707

Spoon River

TOULON is the county seat of Stark County. There is a courthouse built in 1856 where Lincoln and Douglas spoke. The trail head is approximately 1 mile south of town and has parking, water, and restrooms. To enter Toulon take the road to the right just beyond the trailhead for a quarter mile to Clinton Street. Proceed one mile and then turn left on Franklin to Main St. (Hwy. 17).

Twp Rd 135
500 N
N Valley Rd
400 N
W. Jersey Rd
300 N
Camp Run Creek
County Hwy 3
150 N
Mud Run Creek
75 N

Spoon River

STARK COUNTY
PEORIA COUNTY
County Line Rd
N Cedar Bluff Rd

Streitmatter Rd

MATCH   LINE

OTHER FEATURES OF THE ROCK ISLAND TRAIL INCLUDE:

An arched culvert with wing wall construction of massive limestone blocks, located about 2 miles north of Alta. A steel trestle bridge, circa 1910, spanning the Spoon River. A rehabilitated rail station in Wyoming, which was built in 1871.

ROUTES

━━━ Bicycling Trail
━━━ Roadway

FACILITIES

🔧 Bike Repair
❓ Info
🅿 Parking
🚻 Picnic
🚻 Restrooms
🚰 Water
MF Multi Facilities Available

Refreshments   First Aid
Telephone   Picnic
Restrooms   Lodging

PRINCEVILLE You cross the Santa Fe railroad tracks as you enter the town from the south. Just beyond the tracks is a park with restrooms and a picnic area. The trail connects through city streets- proceed on Walnut to North Ave. a short distance and left onto North Town Rd. for a half mile. Turn left on a marked single lane road to connect with the trail again.

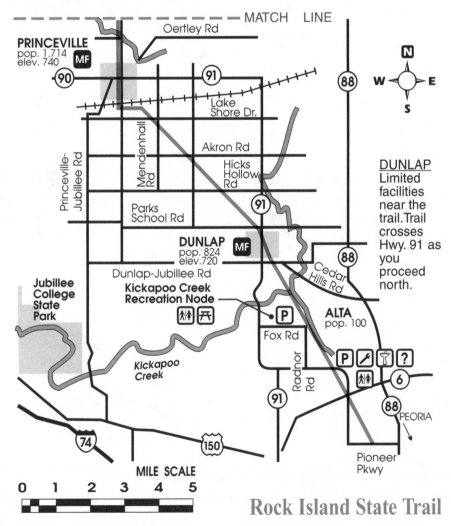

DUNLAP Limited facilities near the trail. Trail crosses Hwy. 91 as you proceed north.

Rock Island State Trail

Salt Creek Bicycle Trail

Trail Length	6.6 miles
Surface	Paved
Uses	Leisure bicycling, cross country skiing, jogging
Location & Setting	Located in west central Cook County. Bordered clockwise by the communities of Oakbrook, Westchester, Brookfield, LaGrange Park, LaGrange and Hinsdale. The Salt Creek Trail starts in Bemis Woods South and continues east to Brookfield Woods, directly across from the Brookfield Zoo. As the trail follows Salt Creek, it provides access to various picnic groves and other points of interest. The trail may be accessed from Ogden Avenue, just east of Wolf Road, or from 31st Street between First Avenue and Prairie Avenue.
Information	Forest Preserve District of Cook County (708) 366-9420 536 N. Harlem Avenue River Forest, IL 60305 Emergency Assistance Forest Preserve Police (708) 366-8210
County	Cook

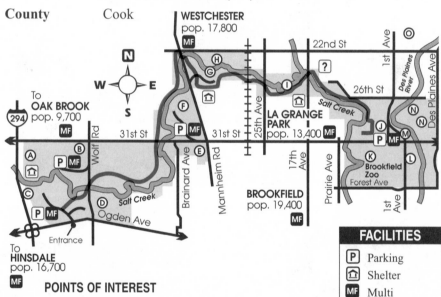

POINTS OF INTEREST

A. Meadow Lark Golf Course
B. Bemis Woods North
C. Bemis Woods South
D. Salt Creek Nursery
E. La Grange Park Woods
F. Possum Hollow Woods
G. Brezina Woods
H. Westchester Woods

I. 26th Street Woods
J. Brookfield Woods
K. Brookfield Zoo
L. Zoo Woods
M. McCormick Woods
N. National Grove-North & South
O. Miller Meadows

FACILITIES

P Parking
Shelter
MF Multi Facilities Available

Refreshments   First Aid
Telephone   Picnic
Restrooms   Lodging

Sterne's Woods Bicycle Trail

Trail Length	Approximately 2.0 miles	
Surface	Dirt road	
Uses	Fat tire bicycling, cross country skiing, hiking	
Location & Setting	Located on the north side of Crystal Lake. Access from Hillside Road or connect from Veteran Acres Park.	
Information	Crystal Lake Park District	(815) 459-0680
	One East Crystal Lake Avenue	
	Crystal Lake, IL 60014	
County	McHenry	

ROUTES

Bicycling Trail
Roadway

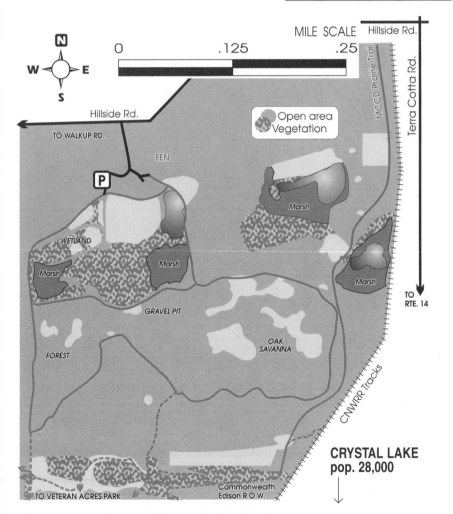

MILE SCALE   Hillside Rd.

0   .125   .25

N   W   E   S

Hillside Rd.

TO WALKUP RD.

FEN

P

Open area
Vegetation

Marsh

WETLAND

Marsh

Marsh

Marsh

GRAVEL PIT

OAK
SAVANNA

FOREST

MCCD Prairie Trail

Terra Cotta Rd.

TO
RTE. 14

CNWRR Tracks

CRYSTAL LAKE
pop. 28,000

TO VETERAN ACRES PARK

Commonwealth
Edison R.O.W.

Stone Bridge Trail

Trail Length	5.75 miles
Surface	Screenings
Uses	Leisure bicycling, cross country skiing, jogging, snowmobiling
Location & Setting	The trail is built on an abandoned railbed and begins at McCurry Road in Roscoe then proceeds southeast to the Boone county line. The setting is rural with wide open areas and farmland.
Information	Rockford Park District
	1401 N. Second Street
	Rockford, IL 61107-3086
County	Winnebago

(815) 987-8865

Plans include the joining of the Stone Bridge Trail with the Long Prairie Trail in Boone County.

ROUTES

Bicycling Trail
Planned Trail
Roadway

FACILITIES

P Parking

MF Multi Facilities Available

Refreshments
Telephone
Restrooms
First Aid
Picnic
Lodging

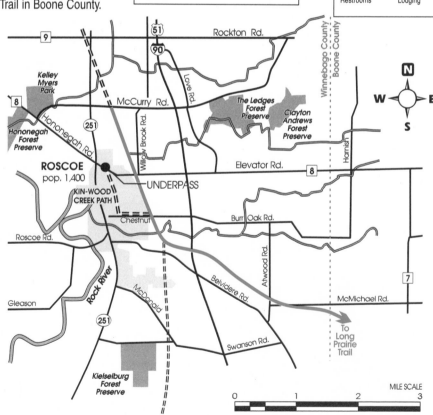

Thorn Creek Forest Preserve

Trail Length	8.0 miles
Surface	Paved
Uses	Leisure bicycling, cross country skiing, jogging
Location & Setting	The Thorn Creek Bicycle Trail is located in far south Cook County. One section consists of trail through the Sauk Trail lake area and another winds through Lansing Woods and North Creek Meadow. A future extension will link these sections. Access the western section along Ashland Avenue, and the eastern section from either Glenwood-Lansing Road or 183rd Street east of Torrence Avenue. It is bounded clockwise by the communities of South Holland, Lansing, Chicago Heights, South Chicago Heights, Park Forest, Olympia Fields, Glenwood and Thornton.
Information	Forest Preserve District of Cook County (708) 366-9420 536 N. Harlem Avenue River Forest, IL 60305
	Emergency Assistance Forest Preserve Police (708) 366-8210
County	Cook

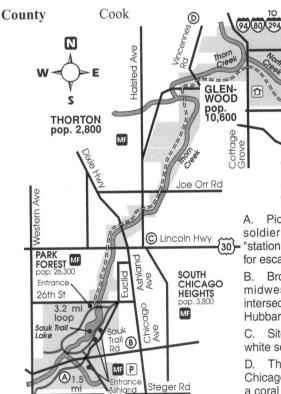

A.   Pioneer homesite of John McCoy, soldier in the Revolutionary War; a "station" on the "Underground Railroad" for escaped slaves.

B.   Brown's Corners- a crossroads of midwest America in pioneer days-intersection of the Great Sauk Trail with Hubbard's Trace to Danville.

C.   Site of Absalom Well's cabin- first white settler in this part of Cook County.

D.   Thornton quarry, largest in the Chicago region, is notable for fossils and a coral reef in the Niagara limestone.

Tinley Creek Forest Preserve

Trail Length	18.5 miles
Surface	Paved
Uses	Leisure bicycling, cross country skiing, jogging
Location & Setting	The Tinley Creek Bicycle Trail is located in southwestern Cook County. The trail passes through gently rolling country, forests, prairies and alongside wetlands. It is bordered (clockwise) by the communities of Palos Heights, Crestwood, Oak Forest, Country Club Hills, Flossmoor, Tinley Park and Orland Park.
Information	Forest Preserve District of Cook County (708) 366-9420 536 N. Harlem Avenue River Forest, IL 60305 Emergency Assistance Forest Preserve Police (708) 366-8210
County	Cook

Pause along 159th Street, just east of Oak Park Avenue, for an unusual view of the Chicago skyline, approximately 20 miles to the northeast. There are accesses and parking along Central Avenue between 159th Street and 175th Street in the northern section. Access and parking to the southern loop is available off both Vollmer and Flossmoor Roads. A future extension will link these two sections.

A. Arrowhead Lake Access Area
B. Elizabeth A. Conkey Forest
C. Turtlehead Lake Access Area
D. Rubio Woods
E. The George W. Dunne National Golf Course
F. Yankee Woods
G. Midlothian Reservoir (Twin Lakes)
H. Midlothian Meadows
I. St. Mihiel West
J. Vollmer Road Picnic

Vadalabene Nature Trail

Trail Length	7.4 miles
Surface	Asphalt (12 feet wide)
Uses	Leisure bicycling, hiking, in-line skating
Location & Setting	Located between Esic Drive in Edwardsville and Lake Drive, east of Granite City. It goes through the Southern Illinois University campus. Setting is rural, with farmland, open areas, woods. The communities at either trailhead have full service facilities.
Information	Madison County Transit Authority (800) 628-7433 1 Transit Way Granite City, IL 62040
County	Madison

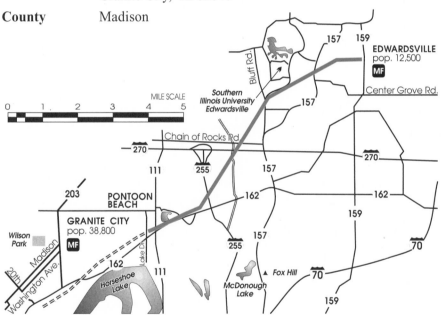

FACILITIES

+	First Aid
🛏	Lodging
P	Parking
MF	Multi Facilities Available

Refreshments   First Aid
Telephone   Picnic
Restrooms   Lodging

When completed, the trail will extend from the Market Basket in Edwardsville to Washington Avenue in Granite City. This trail is isolated. It should be used only in groups and in daylight.

ROUTES

Bicycling Trail
Planned Trail
Roadway

Vadalabene River Road Bikeway

Trail Length	19 miles
Surface	Paved
Uses	Leisure bicycling, hiking
Location & Setting	This path follows Route 100 between Alton, through Grafton and to Pere Marquette State Park. The bikeway is bordered by towering limestone cliffs and the Mississippi River, and is a recreational destination for bicycle enthusiasts.
Information	Illinois Dept. of Transportation (618) 346-3100 1100 Eastport Plaza Drive Collinsville, IL 62234 Southern Illinois Tourism Council Box 286—Belleville, IL 62222
County	Madison, Jersey

ROUTES

▬▬ Bicycling Trail
▬▬ Roadway

9
Powerline Rd.
To Pere Marquette
3
GRAFTON pop. 1,024
100
ELSAH pop. 990
3
267
Pierce
GODFREY
100
PORTAGE DES SIOUX
Mississippi River
3
67
ALTON pop. 34,200
111
MISSOURI
140
94
100
Hospital
143
67
WEST ALTON

N
W—E
S

FACILITIES

+ First Aid
🛏 Lodging
P Parking
MF Multi Facilities Available

Refreshments   First Aid
Telephone   Picnic
Restrooms   Lodging

The northern section follows the wide paved shoulders of the McAdams Parkway to Grafton. The southern section is a separate paved path built on an abandoned railroad line at the base of the bluffs. There are parking areas along and at each end of the bikeway. Pause to visit the historic town of Grafton and Elsah with their antique shops.

Vernon Hills Trails

	Century Park	**Deerpath**
Trail Length	2.9 miles (loops)	1.25 miles
Surface	Paved	
Uses	Leisure bicycling, in-line skating, cross country skiing, hiking/jogging	

Location & Setting	Vernon Hills is located in central Lake County.	
	Century Park	**Deerpath**
	Route 60 west of Route 21 to Lakeview Parkway. Turn north for ½ mile to the park.	Route 21 (Milwaukee Avenue) past Lakeview Parkway to Deerpath Drive. Turn south and proceed to Cherokee Road. Turn east (left) to Deerpath Park.

Information	Vernon Hills Park District	(847) 367-7270
	610 Cherry Valley Road	
	Vernon Hills, IL 60061	

County	Lake

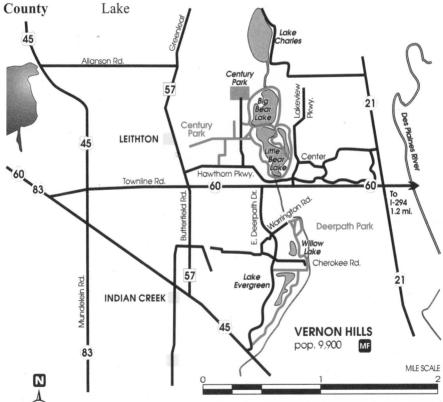

Open field and some woods. Exercise stations surround the lake in Century Park. The path runs through Deerpath Park playgrounds, tennis courts and a small lake.

Veteran Acres Park

Trail Length	Approximately 7.5 miles
Surface	Natural
Uses	Fat tire bicycling, cross country skiing, hiking
Location & Setting	Located on the north side of Crystal Lake. Access from Terra Cotta Road from the south or Walkup Road from the west.
Information	Crystal Lake Park District (815) 459-0680 One East Crystal Lake Avenue Crystal Lake, IL 60014
County	McHenry

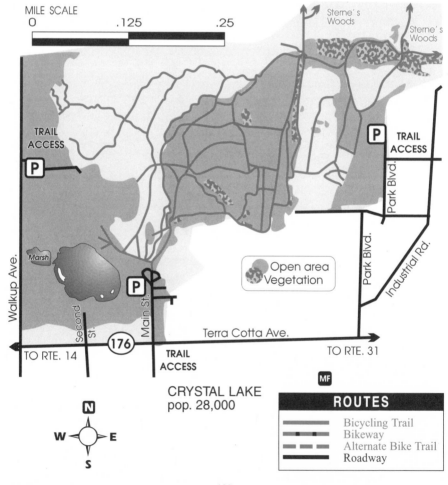

MILE SCALE

0   .125   .25

TRAIL ACCESS

P

TRAIL ACCESS

P

Sterne's Woods

Sterne's Woods

Park Blvd.

Park Blvd.

Industrial Rd.

Walkup Ave.

Marsh

Second St.

Main St.

P

Open area
Vegetation

Terra Cotta Ave.

176

TO RTE. 14

TRAIL ACCESS

TO RTE. 31

CRYSTAL LAKE
pop. 28,000

N
W   E
S

MF

ROUTES

Bicycling Trail
Bikeway
Alternate Bike Trail
Roadway

Virgil L. Gilman Nature Trail

🚴 ⛷ 🚶

Trail Length	10.5 miles
Surface	Paved
Uses	Leisure bicycling, cross country skiing, hiking
Location & Setting	The trail stretches west uninterrupted past farmlands straddling the Kane and Kendall County border. The Virgil Gilman Trail passes rural, urban and suburban areas.
Information	*Kane County Forest Preserve* *(630) 232-1242* Fox River Park District (630) 897-0516 712 South River Aurora, IL 60507
County	Kane

The rural landscape gives way to city life when entering Aurora.

MILE SCALE
0   1   2

SUGAR GROVE pop. 2,000

The trail will extend through Bliss Woods to Waubonsee College.

FACILITIES

🚲	Bike Repair
✚	First Aid
🛏	Lodging
P	Parking
⛱	Picnic
🚻	Restrooms
MF	Multi Facilities Available

Refreshments   First Aid
Telephone   Picnic
Restrooms   Lodging

Aurora is the largest community in Kane County. It was the first midwest community to electrically illuminate its streets.

Services are available at Parker Avenue, Elmwood Drive, Orchard Road, Blackberry Village and Bliss Woods.

ON STREET ROUTE

Terry Ave — Elmwood Dr — Ridgeway — Lake St — Rathbone — Copley Park

Waterfall Glen Forest Preserve

Trail Length 8.5 miles (developed)

Surface Limestone screenings

Uses Leisure and fat tire bicycling, cross country skiing, hiking

Location & Setting Southeast corner of DuPage County, the trail circles Argonne National Laboratory. Forests, prairie, open areas.

Information Forest Preserve District of DuPage County (630) 790-4900
185 Spring Avenue
Glen Ellyn, IL 60138

County DuPage

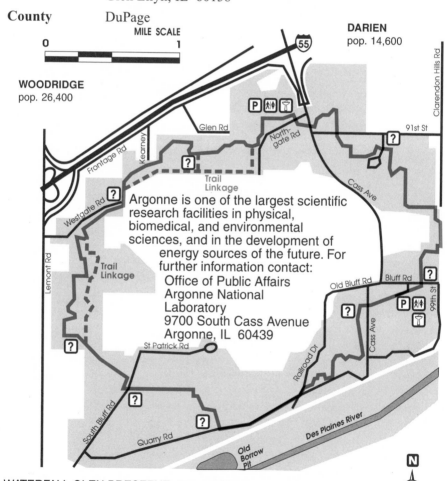

MILE SCALE

0   1

WOODRIDGE
pop. 26,400

DARIEN
pop. 14,600

Argonne is one of the largest scientific research facilities in physical, biomedical, and environmental sciences, and in the development of energy sources of the future. For further information contact:
Office of Public Affairs
Argonne National Laboratory
9700 South Cass Avenue
Argonne, IL 60439

Trail Linkage

Glen Rd • Northgate Rd • Kearney • Frontage Rd • Westgate Rd • Lemont Rd • St Patrick Rd • South Bluff Rd • Quarry Rd • Old Borrow Pit • Railroad Dr • Old Bluff Rd • Bluff Rd • Cass Ave • 99th St • 91st St • Clarendon Hills Rd • Des Plaines River

N
W — E
S

<u>WATERFALL GLEN PRESERVE</u> Waterfall Glen provides some of the best bicycling, cross country skiing and hiking in DuPage County. The main trail is 8 feet wide. In addition, there are many mowed grass trails and footpaths through the preserve.

Zion Bicycle Path

Trail Length	6.5 miles
Surface	Paved
Uses	Leisure bicycling, in-line skating, jogging
Location & Setting	This bicycle path and bikeway is located in the community of Zion in far northeastern Illinois. The setting is surburban.
Information	Zion Park District (847) 746-5500 2400 Dowie Memorial Drive Zion, IL 60099
County	Lake

ROUTES

- ━━━ Bicycling Trail
- ▬ ▬ Bikeway
- ▬ ▬ Alternate Bike Trail
- ━━━ Roadway

There is a trail extension planned that will run west along the Commonwealth Edison right-of-way (near Hwy. 173) to the Highland Meadows development.

FACILITIES

- [?] Info
- [P] Parking
- [🎋] Picnic
- [⑪] Refreshments
- [👫] Restrooms
- [🚰] Water
- [MF] Multi Facilities Available

Refreshments   First Aid
Telephone   Picnic
Restrooms   Lodging

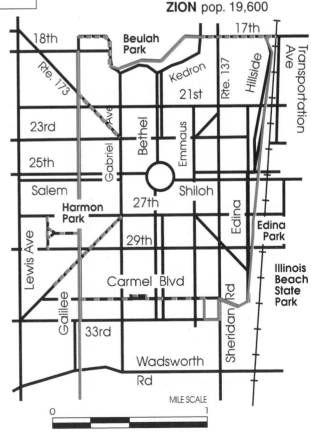

ZION pop. 19,600

MILE SCALE

0   1

Selected Illinois State Parks
North West Region

North West Region Park Name	Acreage	Concession	Drinking Water	Rest rooms	Bike Trails	Boat Rentals	Canoe Access	Canoe Rental	Hiking	Camping
Argyle Lake State Park	1700	●	●	♿		●	●		●	AB/CDY
Big River State Forest	3027		♿	♿			●		●	CD
Castle Rock State Park	1995		●	●			●		●	Canoe
Delabar State Park	89		●	●			●		●	B/ECD
Hennepin Canal Parkway State Park	5773		♿	♿	●		●		♿	CDY
Ilini State Park	510	●	●	♿			●		●	B/ECY
Johnson-Sauk Trail State Park	1361	●	♿	♿		●	●		●	B/E♿DY
Jubilee College State Park	3500		♿	♿					●	AB/SC♿
Lake Le-Aqua-Na State Park	715	●	●	♿		●	●		♿	AB/SCY
Lowden State Park	2234	●	♿	♿					●	AB/SD
Mississippi Palisades State Park	2505	●	●	♿			●		●	AB/SDY
Rock Cut State Park	3092	●	♿	♿	●	●	●		●	A♿B/SCY
Rock Island Trail State Park	392		♿	♿	●				●	D
Starved Rock State Park	2630	♿	♿	♿			●		●	A♿YL
White Pines Forest State Park	385	♿	●	♿					●	CY

CLASS **A** SITES Showers, electricity & vehicular access *(fee)*

CLASS **B/E** SITES Electricity & vehicular access *(fee)*

CLASS **B/S** SITES Showers & vehicular access *(fee)*

CLASS **C** SITES Vehicular access *(fee)*

CLASS **D** SITES Tent camping/primitive sites (walk in/backpack) no vehicular access *(fee)*

CLASS **Y** SITES Youth Groups only

♿ Accessible to visitors with disabilities

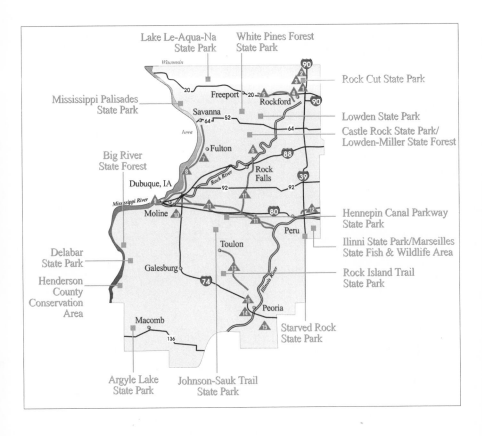

Illinois State Parks
North West Region

North East Region

North East Region Park Name	FACILITIES				ACTIVITIES					
	Acreage	Concession	Drinking Water	Rest rooms	Bike Trails	Boat Rentals	Canoe Access	Canoe Rental	Hiking	Camping
Chain O'Lakes State Park	6063	●	&	&	●	●	●	●		AB/SY
Channahon State Park	25		●	●	●		●		●	DY
Des Plaines Conservation Area	5012	●	●	&			●		●	C
Gebhard Woods State Park	30		&	●			●		●	DY
Goose Lake Prairie State Nat'l. Area	2468		●	&					●	
I & M Canal State Trail	2802		●	●	●		●		●	D
Illinois Beach State Park	4160	&	&	&	●		●		&	A&YL
Kankakee River State Park	3932	&	&	&	●		●	●	●	A&B/ECDY
Moraine Hills State Park	1763	●	&	●	●	●			●	
Silver Springs State Park	1314	●	●	&			●	●	●	DY

CLASS **A** SITES	Showers, electricity & vehicular access *(fee)*
CLASS **B/E** SITES	Electricity & vehicular access *(fee)*
CLASS **B/S** SITES	Showers & vehicular access *(fee)*
CLASS **C** SITES	Vehicular access *(fee)*
CLASS **D** SITES	Tent camping/primitive sites (walk in/backpack) no vehicular access *(fee)*
CLASS **Y** SITES	Youth Groups only
&	Accessible to visitors with disabilities

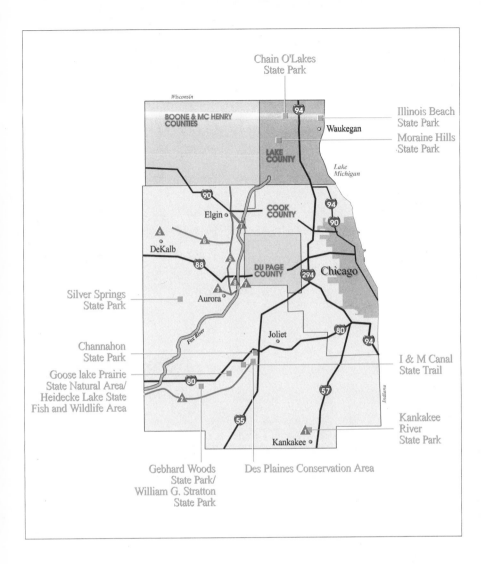

No.	Trail Name	Page #
1.)	Kankakee River State Park	70
2.)	I & M Canal State Trail	63
3.)	Virgil L. Gilman Nature Trail	105
4.)	Peace Road Trail	83
5.)	Fox River Trail	43
6.)	Great Western Trail	51
7.)	Illinois Prairie Path	68
8.)	Fermilab Bike Trail	42

Illinois State Parks
North East Region

East Central Region

East Central Region — Park Name	Acreage	FACILITIES Concession	FACILITIES Drinking Water	FACILITIES Rest rooms	ACTIVITIES Bike Trails	ACTIVITIES Boat Rentals	ACTIVITIES Canoe Access	ACTIVITIES Canoe Rental	ACTIVITIES Hiking	ACTIVITIES Camping
Clinton Lake State Recreation Area	9915		♿	♿			•		•	B/SY
Eagle Creek State Recreation Area	1463		•	♿					•	B/ECY
Fox Ridge State Park	1517		•	♿					•	B/SY
Hidden Springs State Forest	1121		•	♿					•	CY
Kickapoo State Park	2844	•	•	♿	•	•	•	•	•	AB/SCDYR
Lincoln Trail State Park	1022	♿	•	♿		•	•	•	•	A♿DY
Moraine View State Park	1688	♿	♿	♿		•	•		♿	B/ED
Walnut Point State Fish & Wildlife Area	592	•	•	♿		•	•		•	B/EDY
Weldon Springs State Park	370	•	•	♿		•	•		•	B/EDY
Wolf Creek State Park	1967		•	♿					•	RACDY

CLASS **A** SITES Showers, electricity & vehicular access *(fee)*

CLASS **B/E** SITES Electricity & vehicular access *(fee)*

CLASS **B/S** SITES Showers & vehicular access *(fee)*

CLASS **C** SITES Vehicular access *(fee)*

CLASS **D** SITES Tent camping/primitive sites (walk in/backpack) no vehicular access *(fee)*

CLASS **Y** SITES Youth Groups only

♿ Accessible to visitors with disabilities

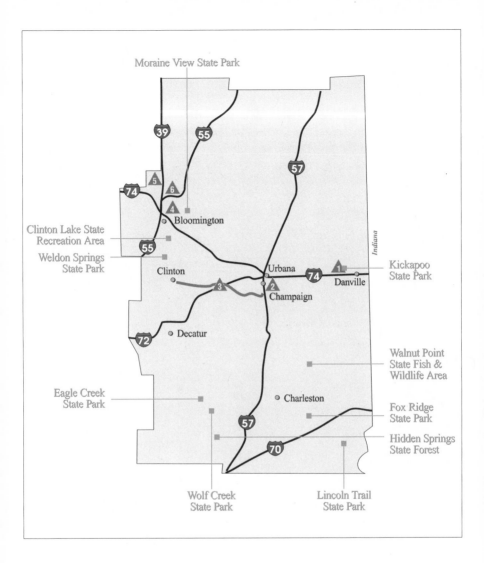

Moraine View State Park

Clinton Lake State Recreation Area

Weldon Springs State Park

Clinton

Bloomington

Urbana

Champaign

Kickapoo State Park

Danville

Indiana

Decatur

Walnut Point State Fish & Wildlife Area

Eagle Creek State Park

Charleston

Fox Ridge State Park

Hidden Springs State Forest

Wolf Creek State Park

Lincoln Trail State Park

Illinois State Parks
East Central Region

Selected Illinois State Parks
West Central & South Regions

West Central and South Region — Park Name	Acreage	Concession	Drinking Water	Rest rooms	Bike Trails	Boat Rentals	Canoe Access	Canoe Rental	Hiking	Camping
FACILITIES		Concession	Drinking Water	Rest rooms	**ACTIVITIES**					
WEST CENTRAL REGION										
Beaver Dam State Park	744	•	•	&		•	•		•	AB/SY
Horseshoe Lake State Park	2854		•	&			•		•	C&
Nauvoo State Park	148		&	&			•		•	B/ECY
Pere Marquette State Park	7901	•	•	&	•				•	A&B/SYL
Randolph County State F & W Area	1021	•	•	&		•	•		•	C&DY
Sand Ridge State Forest	7112		•	•					•	CDY
Sangchris Lake State Park	3576	•		&			•			B/ECDY
Siloam Springs State Park	3323	&	&	&		•	•		•	A&B/SD
Washington County Conservation Area	1440	&	&	&		•	•		•	A&CY
Weinberg-King State Park	772		•	&					•	C&Y
SOUTH REGION										
Cave-in-Rock State Park	204	•	•	&			•		•	B/ECDY
Dixon Springs State Park	787	&	&	&				•	•	B/ED&Y
Ferne Clyffe State Park	1125		&	&					•	ADY
Fort Massac State Park	1499		&	&			•		•	A&B/S
Giant City State Park	3694	&	&	&			•	•	&	A&DYL
Hamilton County Conservation Area	1683	•	•	•		•	•		•	B/EDY
Horseshoe Lake Conservation Area	9550		&	&			•			A&B/EC
Lake Murphysboro State Park	1024	&	•	&		•	•		•	A/ECY
Pyramid State Park	2528		•	•			•		•	CD
Ramsey Lake State Park	1881	•	•	&		•	•		•	AB,ECDY
Red Hills State Park	948	•	•	&		•	•		•	A&DY
Sam Dale Lake Conservation Area	1301	•	&	&		•	•		•	B/ED&Y
Sam Parr State Park	1133		•	•			•		•	CDY
Trail of Tears State Forest	4993		•	•					•	DCY
Wayne Fitzgerrell State Park	3300	•	•	•		•		•	•	AD

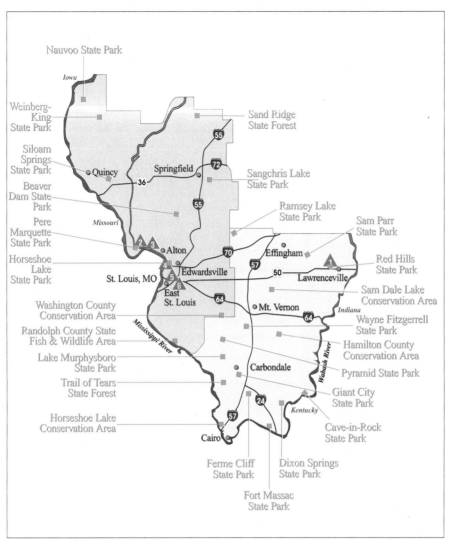

CLASS **A** SITES	Showers, electricity & vehicular access *(fee)*
CLASS **B/E** SITES	Electricity & vehicular access *(fee)*
CLASS **B/S** SITES	Showers & vehicular access *(fee)*
CLASS **C** SITES	Vehicular access *(fee)*
CLASS **D** SITES	Tent camping/primitive sites (walk in/backpack) no vehicular access *(fee)*
CLASS **Y** SITES	Youth Groups only
♿	Accessible to visitors with disabilities

Illinois State Parks West Central & South Regions

INDEX

(Continued on next page)

CITY TO TRAIL INDEX

CITY	TRAIL	PAGE NO.

(Continued on next page)

CITY TO TRAIL INDEX (CONTINUED)

(Continued on next page)

(Continued on next page)

City to Trail Index (Continued)

County to Trail Index

(Continued on next page)

County to Trail Index (Continued)

To order additional copies of this book:

Pay by Check or Credit Card

Mail Check to:

American Bike Trails
1157 South Milwaukee Avenue
Libertyville, IL 60048

Book *(per copy)* $14.95
Handling *(per order)* $2.00
Sales Tax—IL residents *(per copy)* $1.00

To order by Credit Card call (800) 246-4627

American Bike Trails
publishes and distributes maps, books and guides
for the recreational bicyclist. Our trail maps
cover over 250 trails throughout the states of
Illinois, Iowa, Michigan, Minnesota and Wisconsin.

For a free copy of our catalog write to the above address